State of

Palestine

NOW

By Daoud Kuttab

Forward by:

Dr. Varsen Agabakian Shahin

Palestinian Minister of State for
Foreign and Expatriate Affairs

Dedication

To our grandchildren

Yasmeen, Saleem, Dalia, Karam, Daoud, and Ameer

Hope and pray that a thriving democratic, prosperous and independent Palestinian state exists by the time you are adults

Forward by Dr. Varsen Aghabekian Shahin

Minister of State for Foreign Affairs and Expatriates, State of Palestine

I was excited to read the manuscript of Daoud Kuttab's State of Palestine NOW. The book was an-easy-to-read, and the arguments for Palestinian statehood were well explained.

Daoud Kuttab is an accomplished journalist from Jerusalem whose international coverage of the two intifadas was exceptional.

This book full of personal anecdotes, humanizes the Palestinian narrative. It puts it in the right perspective of our people's struggle for their basic rights, the foremost of which is the right of self-determination. An independent Palestinian state on the June 4th, 1967, lines is the key to peace in the Middle East. Every proposal, initiative, or plan that has not included the rights of Palestinians has been doomed.

State of Palestine NOW is not a theoretical book but a practical guide. It provides a road map for countries and leaders worldwide that talks about the two-state solution but do little to translate their words into policy.

The number of world powers that have recognized the state of Palestine has reached three-quarters of the UN member states. Unfortunately, the permanent members of the United Nations Security Council are still hesitant to turn their own public positions of supporting a Palestinian state alongside Israel into the simple but important act of officially recognizing the Palestinian state.

I urge all to read this important book and more importantly, call on all countries to recognize Palestine and for those who already have recognized Palestine, to work with us to ensure that an independent pluralistic and democratic state of Palestinian can emerge as a peaceful and contributing member of the international community. We deserve our potential to be unleashed to focus on materializing the State of Palestine rather than struggling against an emboldened occupation, and to look forward for a better future to all, where justice prevails, and people enjoy peace, security, and stability.

Ramallah, Palestine, December 2024

Introduction

Two days after Hamas's October 7th, 2023, cross border attack that caused hundreds of Israeli military and civilian deaths, and hundreds taken hostage, I wrote an op-ed article in the Washington Post October 9th.

I tried to explain the fact that the explosion that occurred was not without context, pointing out to 75 years that Palestinian refugees (more than half of the residents of Gaza) have been waiting for the fulfillment of their right of return as mandated by UN Resolution 194. I also pointed out the fact that 57 years since the West Bank (including East Jerusalem) and Gaza has been under Israeli occupation in June 1967 and that the Gaza Strip itself has been under an illegal siege for 17 years.

But what I most focused on in the article was the fact that for years the constant Palestinian political cry repeated to all has been the absence of a political horizon. In fact, when US President Joe Biden visited Bethlehem to meet with President Mahmoud

Abbas, the US leader told Palestinians that "the time was not ripe" for an independent state alongside Israel.

In 2024 alone, important new states including Spain, Ireland and Norway as well as the Bahamas, Trinidad and Tobago, Jamaica and Barbados have joined many around the world who have recognized the state of Palestine.

In fact, 146 out of the 190 UN member states have now recognized the state of Palestine, but three permanent members of the UN security council: the US, the UK, and France have yet to do so and at least one, the United States, has hampered the UN Security Council in its efforts to accept the recommendations of the UN General Assembly that had overwhelmingly supported Palestinian statehood.

This book will trace the post-colonial Palestinian aspiration since the beginnings of the 20th century and will provide the arguments for the immediate need for the realization of the state of Palestine NOW.

Jerusalem, Palestine, November 2024

Chapter One

Why an independent state on parts of Palestine?

The Palestinian national movement has historically talked about Palestine as an Arab country. "Falastin Arabiyeh" has been the slogan of Palestinian and Arab demonstrators ever since the post-World War I era. While Palestine was the key to Arab nationalism that took place during the Ottoman era and continued till the post-colonial period in the Arab world, it was the Palestine Liberation Organization (PLO) that was able to translate this aspiration into ideological terms. The PLO charter spoke clearly about the need to remove religion from the political formula and therefore opted for a "secular democratic state" in Palestine for its citizens regardless of their religion or ethnicity. Naturally, since the vast majority of Palestinians were Arab, the issue was not a source of controversy.

The PLO's goal was to liberate Palestine from the Mediterranean Sea to the River Jordan and turn it into this democratic state for its citizens. With the flow of Jewish immigration into Palestine and the rise of the state of Israel, the idea of a secular state ran into a simple but profound problem. While there was no question about the indigenous original Jews that lived in Palestine for ages, the big question was about the new Jews who had come to Palestine in the 20th century, especially in the aftermath of the horrendous holocaust in Europe. Some Palestinian leaders attempted to talk about a cut-off period. Some said that Jews who came after 1930 or after 1948 were not to be included in the aspiration of the secular democratic state.

In their mind, you cannot have a proper democracy if one ethnic/religious group continues to bring its people into the country and change the country's demography. Whereas when the UN voted in the Partition Plan in 1947, Jews were a tiny minority but awarded the majority of the land of Palestine. After the establishment of Israel, new waves of Jewish immigrants flooded the country, further tipping the demographic balance, while 750,000 Palestinians were forced to leave, becoming refugees in Palestine's West Bank and Gaza Strip as well as nearby Jordan, Egypt, Syria, and Lebanon.

The concept of one democratic secular state was therefore constantly being weakened. After the Israeli Knesset passed the Law of Return in 1950, every Jew around the world, defined as any person with at least one Jewish grandparent and their spouses, was granted the right to come and instantly take Israeli citizenship. Meanwhile, Palestinians in the newly established Israel were being demoted to third class citizens – behind Sephardi (Oriental or Arab) Jews and Ashkenazi (European) Jews.

The inability of Palestinian nationalists to answer the question of whether, in their mind, a secular democratic state would include all people who were living in Israel/Palestine made it easy for Zionists to paint the PLO's ideology as being a clear formula for the destruction of Israel. It did not help that the rhetoric of some Arab leaders and media propagandists, especially in Egypt, was hate-filled against Jews and Zionists, with some even calling for throwing the Jews into the sea.

The PLO was therefore painted not only as a terrorist organization, but also as one whose aims were to annihilate the small and only Jewish state whose citizens had escaped the ugliest holocaust that the world had ever witnessed. The information campaign was extremely successful to the degree that Palestinians were unable to even make a small crack in world (especially western) public opinion. When some PLO factions began hijacking planes, the terrorism label was quickly and forcefully attached to all Palestinians.

Slow Palestinian change

It would take the Palestinian movement some time before realizing that they are not being effective in penetrating western minds and certainly not western decision-makers. While the PLO preached armed resistance, most of their actions, in fact, were not against Israelis in Israel/Palestine, but against western targets that were enabling Israel and even against Arab countries.

I was 14 when my parents decided to emigrate to the United States. My uncle on my mother's side lived in Amman, where we spent a few days in January 1970 before departing for New Jersey. Aunt Farida, my mother's sister who had met her husband at our Bethlehem home years earlier, had arranged to provide our family with immigration papers.

There were no Palestinian universities at the time and our parents wanted us to have an opportunity for college education, so the offer to go to the US was difficult to refuse. As we waited in Amman to travel, it was clear that PLO fighters were gaining ground, filling the streets of the Jordanian capital, asking for donations, and using the vast advantage they had of working in a country with a large Palestinian population. I remember seeing the Palestinian fedayeen (fighters) in military gear, and as a child looking at them with awe that they would somehow liberate Palestine. A couple of years earlier, the Palestinians and Jordanian military fended off an Israel incursion into the East Bank town of Karameh (which means dignity in Arabic). The PLO, especially Fatah, was able to turn that 21 March 1968 battle into a major source of recruitment. Posters by Yasser Arafat's Fatah movement were quickly produced, celebrating the victory over the invading Israeli soldiers and playing up the name of the town as the sign that Palestinians are fighting for the dignity of all Arabs.

Unlike Fatah, left-wing Palestinian factions, like those of the Arab nationalist Popular Front for the Liberation of Palestine (PFLP) headed by a surgeon refugee from Lydda George Habash, were at loggerheads with the Jordanians in their belief that the road to liberating Jerusalem needed to go through Zahran (the royal Jordanian palace.) PFLP fighters succeeded in hijacking a TWA plane and forcing it to land in the Jordanian desert.

In the end, no one was killed, but the incident poisoned the air. By the fall of 1970, a civil war had broken out between Palestinians and Jordanians, which led to bloodshed and the exit of the PLO from Jordan to Lebanon.

At this time, the PFLP splintered and a new less radical, yet left-wing Democratic Front for the Liberation of Palestine (DFLP) faction was established and headed by a Jordanian patriot, Nayef Hawatmeh. The new group quickly attracted many intellectuals and in 1973, the DFLP declared a 10-point plan that called for Palestinians to set up a state in any part of historic Palestine from which the Israelis would withdraw.

Although the DFLP's 10-point plan constituted a clear retreat from the river to the sea one-state solution, Israeli propagandists attacked the plan as being no different from the effort to annihilate Israel. The only difference that the Israel hasbara (the Hebrew term for propagandist) spread was that the DFLP plan called for Israel's destruction in stages rather than at one time.

When I finished my college education in the US and returned to Jerusalem, I started meeting some of the DFLP thinkers and learning from them about this 10-point plan, which the PLO would later adopt.

But the learning curve for me developed during the first Palestinian intifada (1987-1993) as I became a full-fledged journalist, often writing for the western media as well as having become editor of the English-language Palestinian *Al Fajr* weekly.

Sharing power or sharing land

The best lesson I personally learned about the strategic options available to Palestinians was taught to me by a great Palestinian mind. Professor Sari Nusseibeh, who was the brilliant ideologue of the Palestinian intifada era, was my mentor. I had been a schoolmate of Sari's younger brother Hatem when we were both third grade students at the St. George's School on Nablus Road in East Jerusalem. As an editor of *Al Fajr* and also a fixer with major US media outlets, I would often accompany foreign journalists to Sari's parents' home next to the American Colony Hotel, where western journalists often stayed, and near our newspaper office and my brother's law office. It is also across the street from the Nuzha Building, where the Al Quds Television Productions was based and from where we produced the documentary *Palestinian Diaries*, which was aired on BBC4, Holland TV, and other stations.

Sari drilled into my head a simple yet profound concept. The Palestinian Israeli concept, he would often say, can only be resolved by either sharing power or sharing land. Initially, I did not understand what he meant, but with time I realized that this is exactly the one-state, two-state debate that has become popular in political circles. Either Palestinians and Israelis share power in a single state where all citizens have equal rights, or we share the land; in other words, divide historic Palestine into two states – Israel and Palestine with each having sovereignty over their own state.

It was no easy feat for Sari to come up with this plan supporting the sharing of the land, or the two-state solution arrangement. While Sari during the intifada had become convinced of the sharing of the land two-state solution, he would sometimes tinker with the one-state idea especially in Jerusalem. He also tried to suggest different realistic scenarios for some of the concepts that many Palestinians were repeating without thinking through. He once was teaching a course at Bir Zeit University when he suggested to his students that Palestinians who support the secular democratic state should consider joining the Israeli army as part of the push for equal rights within a one-state solution. His theoretical scenario idea was interpreted by some as treason, prompting some students who did not grasp his exercise to get so angry at him that he ended up being physically attacked by hot-headed students. The attacks against Sari had the perfect result within the PLO, as its mainstream *Falastin Al Thawra* newspaper wrote a strong editorial defending Sari, no doubt on orders from Abu Jihad (Khalil al-Wazir), Fatah's number 2 man who was deeply involved in the Palestinian intifada and was assassinated later in his Tunisia home by Israeli army infiltrators from the sea.

Sari also once wrote an article, which we published in *Al Fajr* English, about his search for a nice swimming pool to take his children, only to realize that the best pool existed in the Maale Adummim settlement not far from his Abu Dis home in East Jerusalem. Sari wrote that those who believe in the one-state solution should try out their ideas in Jerusalem.

For Sari and the Palestinian intifada leadership, the idea of one secular democratic state made little sense in the face of a powerful western-backed state of Israel. Continuing the talk about the PLO's plans was a futile exercise that would backfire. Instead, the intifada started pushing for the idea of a Palestinian state alongside rather than instead of Israel. Palestinian demonstrators and leaders began declaring that they were opposed to the Israeli occupation and not the state of Israel within its internationally recognized borders. This became a much more powerful and convincing argument that started to make inroads into the PLO leadership.

Building on the DFLP's 10-point plan, senior PLO officials started to climb down from their high horses of a single secular democratic state and began tinkering with the idea of a Palestinian state, but it would take time for that transition to take place. The intifada certainly sped up the discussions. The idea of a Palestinian declaration of a state based on international law and the once detested UN

Security Council (UNSC) Resolutions 242 and 338 suddenly became acceptable.

For me, sharing the power or sharing the land became part of my speeches and talks to visiting students, journalists, or with any individual or group that wanted to learn more about the Palestinian cause. I would often give Sari credit, but at other times I would widen the concept by saying that what is happening is neither marriage with shared resources and responsibilities nor divorce with separation and separate lives. I would sometimes venture into the worst situation: neither marriage nor divorce but being screwed without the shared lives nor the separate freedoms.

One state again

The Palestinian leadership and most of the Palestinian public had finally bought into the two-state solution, preferring an independent state on 22 percent of Palestine rather than continuing to fight for a one-state solution that the other side totally refused and would not easily agree to. Israel, a nuclear state with a strong economy, military, political cohesion with unabated international support, and a growing religious nationalistic tendency, was hardly ready to give up all that and share power with Palestinians.

The Oslo Accords appeared to begin the gradual process towards a two-state solution, but unfortunately, it did not include enough guarantees that would ensure that the path to Palestinian statehood was unstoppable. Instead, radical Jewish zealots – including Benjamin Netanyahu's inciting rhetoric – as well as Hamas succeeded in derailing the Oslo Accords. The fact that the accords didn't include a clear suspension of settlements was perhaps the worst blunder committed although at the time, Palestinian negotiators were so convinced that an independent Palestinian state was on its way within five years that they allowed this fatal error to occur. This grave mistake has resulted in the fact that illegal Jewish settlements have more than quadrupled in the West Bank and East Jerusalem since the signing of the Memorandum of Principles outside the White House in September 1993.

The assassination of then-Israeli Prime Minister Yitzhak Rabin by Jewish radical Yigal

Amir, literally on the eve of another Israeli withdrawal in November 1995, had given Shimon Peres a huge spike in the polls. But Peres lost by a very small margin, in part due to the anger of Palestinian citizens of Israel over the shelling by the Israeli forces of Arab (Lebanese and Palestinian) civilians. The attack resulted in the death of 106 civilians who had taken refuge in a UN shelter in the southern Lebanese village of Qana in April 1996, which caused the death of 106 Lebanese and Palestinian civilians.

Netanyahu won elections for the first time in 1996, and with the exception of a short period of Ehud Barak and Ehud Olmert's administration, Bibi, as the Israeli right-wing leader is often called, has been in charge longer than any other Israeli prime minister. He has worked tirelessly, although often behind the scenes, to demolish all efforts at negotiating a peace agreement that would include an independent state while strongly supporting the Jewish settlement movement in the occupied Palestinian territories.

The failure of the Oslo Accords, which also included my arrest and detention for one week by the Palestinian government for fighting corruption, led many to abandon the idea of the two-state solution and revert back to the original Palestinian concept of one state with equal rights.

Even my adult children, especially my son Bishara, began arguing with me to try to convince me to give up on the two-state solution, pointing to the exponential growth of Jewish settlements, the impossibility of a contiguous independent Palestinian state, and scoffing at the idea that any Israeli leader from the left or right would ever give up Jerusalem for peace. I tried to counter that this idea of a single binational state is not doable and certainly not in my lifetime.

But young Palestinians as well as many academics were so frustrated with the inept Palestinian leadership, especially after Arafat's death, that they began fighting for the idea of one state with equal rights.

It was clear to me that based on the balance of power between Palestinians and Israel, it would be very difficult, if not impossible, to get any action going to end the Israeli occupation, whether we replace the Israeli occupation with a one- state plan with equal rights or the two-state solution that will include a Palestinian state.

The effects of 7 October on the balance of power

Then the 7 October 2023 cross-border raid by Hamas from Gaza happened, shaking the geopolitical foundations of the region and possibly the rest of the world. One can easily argue that the Palestinian cause after 7 October is certainly not the same as it was before, creating new facts on the ground. The main fact is that the invisible Israeli war machine was proven to be vulnerable and a war on multiple fronts – with Lebanon, West Bank, Gaza, Yemen, and even some attacks from Iraq and a couple of unprecedented drone and missile strikes from Iran – would stretch the Israeli defensive strategy to its limits. The fact that a group of Palestinians under a 17-year siege were able to take even one hostage and withstand a brutal genocidal attack that spared no one and included the weapon of starvation would not produce a surrender was perhaps unthinkable. If one would merely remember that in 1967, Israel occupied the Sinai, Gaza Strip, the West Bank, and the Golan Heights in only six days but has been unable to defeat Palestinian resistance fighters in Gaza for more than a year, the fact that the balance of power is changing could only stare you in the face.

While Israel violated all rules to continue its indiscriminate attacks and siege and prevented foreign media from entering Gaza, still the war on Gaza, with the high human cost of the Israeli carnage, has revived the Palestinian cause like no other event. The protests of American university students, including at the prestigious Ivy League colleges, showed that the justice of the Palestinian cause and the struggle against settler colonialism cannot be shut down or drowned out no matter what.

With world attention for the cause of Palestine rising, the one-state idea captured the imagination of many, especially young people and academics, while western countries that had been giving lip service to the two-state solution realized that they needed to do more to support and recognize the Palestinian state while encouraging the

Israelis to give up their occupation, whether through negotiations or unilaterally. The International Court of Justice and the International Criminal Court became busy fielding complaints from various countries and organizations around the world demanding Israel's accountability for its war crimes, genocide, and apartheid policies.

Young demonstrators in many parts of the world took to the streets calling "Free free Palestine" and demanding that Palestinians be "free from the River to the Sea" in clear-cut support for the equal rights idea within a one-state solution.

Debate

I was on a family visit to Philadelphia in the spring of 2024 when my younger brother Sam, who has been active in Palestinian circles in the US for decades, invited me to attend a Ramadan iftar (fast-breaking meal during the Muslim fasting month) at a local mosque. Sam had begun an interfaith activity outside many churches along with other Arab and Jewish Americans who were asking American churches to pray for Gaza.

The keynote speaker at that Ramadan event I was invited to and attended turned out to be my cousin Mubarak Awad, who had come to Philadelphia along with Michael Beer, the director of the Nonviolence International Center in Washington D.C. Also, at the *iftar* was my older brother Jonathan, an international lawyer who had established along with Palestinian lawyer Raja Shehadeh the Al Haq human rights center in the 1980s and was working in the US at the time trying to change minds of some of the American Christian Zionists who were supportive of Israel and basing their support on warped biblical interpretations.

I was so happy to see Mubarak again, having always been one of my role models from the days he was a boxing champion in the West Bank, to the days he convinced many Palestinians during the 1967 war not to leave their homes, and his nonviolence advocacy in the years preceding the Palestinian intifada.

Nonviolence International published a book written by Jonathan entitled *Beyond the Two-State Solution* in three languages (English, Hebrew, and Arabic). Even though Jonathan was the legal advisor to the Palestinian negotiating team in Cairo during the Oslo Accords talks, he had turned sour on the two-state solution and became an advocate of equal rights within one state. His book outlines the reasons why many Palestinians have abandoned the two-state solution and provides practical ideas on how the one-state solution could overcome many of the problems that exist today with the dangerously considerable increase of Jewish settlers in the West Bank, the problems in Jerusalem around Al Aqsa Mosque, and the fact that Palestinian are disenfranchised living under what appears to be a never-ending occupation.

Michael Beer had been clearly reading a lot of my writings, including the 9 October *Washington Post* article explaining how the explosion occurred due to the absence of a political horizon and that the solution lies in the establishment of a Palestinian state.

Noting that the two brothers were on opposite sides of the issue, Michael suggested a debate between the brothers, and we both agreed immediately. It would take a while to produce the Zoom debate, but the results in terms of followers, viewers, and the discussion that ensued have been quite powerful.

The debate on 28 July 2024 was civil and pleasant. We exchanged ideas and each defended his point of view. I am not sure who won the debate, but many of the people I have spoken with since have told me that the conversation opened up their eyes to many issues. While many said that they supported the one-state solution, they accepted my argument that what is needed is not this or that solution, but a plan that can end the occupation. My argument that Palestine must be an independent state even for one day and then the people of Palestine can decide whether they want to confederate or federate with either Israel or Jordan or stay as a Palestinian state resonated with those I spoke to.

Somehow, many supporters of the one-state solution expect it to be a Palestinian Arab state. They have not thought through what kind of state it would be when decisions and powers are shared with most likely unrepentant racist Jews. Another more important aspect is that almost all realize that the one-state solution is not feasible any time soon, but some people are still clinging to it because they are unhappy with the current Palestinian leadership, or they feel that the one-state solution is the more sustainable plan in the long term.

The added attention to Palestine has also caused some supporters of the one-state solution to rethink their position for varied reasons. After seeing the brutality and inhumanity of Israelis, many are wondering how we can live with such people who have shown zero humanity towards women and children in Gaza. Others are realizing that changes around the world and the decisions of the world courts in favor of the right of Palestinian self-determination constitute a huge once-in-a-lifetime opportunity that must be grabbed before Israel can recoup and the world again loses interest in Palestinian rights.

The debate with Jonathan pushed me to write this book with the hope that I can further elaborate not only on the current viability of the two-state solution but also to dig into the arguments and counterarguments often presented by Israel and its protagonists in their opposition to a Palestinian state. In fact, the decision in mid-July 2024 by the Israeli Knesset opposing a Palestinian state, which was followed two days later on 19 July by a powerful ruling of the International Court of Justice in favor of the right of Palestinians to self-determination and the right to an independent state, makes the idea not only viable but necessary to be accepted and defended.

The idea of a Palestinian state on part of Palestine might be seen by many as a historic compromise, but after decades of suffering, it is the right way out of the decades of foreign occupation, Jewish colonialism, and Jewish supremacy to non-Jews throughout historic Palestine. This is a realistic and doable solution for now. Once Palestinians can establish and exercise their right of self-determination on their own land, it becomes possible for future generations of Palestinians and Israelis to see the light and the value of working together, potentially creating a single state with equal rights the way that Europeans were able to work out their problems after the world wars. For now, the goal and the compass of Palestinians and lovers of Palestine must be focused on the realization of an independent state of Palestine on the 4 June 1967 borders.

Chapter Two

Historic look at the term 'Palestine'

Much has been written and argued about the land between the River Jordan and the Mediterranean Sea. Jews who had short term kingdoms in part of Palestine claim that they have a historic, and even God-given, right to the land, whereas Palestinians make the same claim based on continuously living on the land for millennia.

What has been missing in the discussions is what the term 'Palestine' refers to. While today's Palestinian population is ethnically Arab of mostly Muslims, Christians, and other faiths, for Palestinians, the term 'Palestine' is not an exclusive one for any particular national or religious affiliation.

Palestine for Palestinians encompasses all who are living on this land and the term includes all ethnicities, religious affiliations, and nationalities. So, even though the majority of today's Palestinians are Muslim Arabs, the term 'Palestinians' includes various members of Arab/Muslim dynasties, such as the Ayyubids and the Canaanite Jebusites, but it also includes Jews. The PLO proudly includes a number of Jewish Palestinians such as Uri Davis, a member of the Revolutionary Council of the PLO's main faction, Fatah.

From the beginning of time, Palestine was trodden by occupiers and rulers. Some of them have left their mark on the land and whose descendants can be seen among today's population; others have long been forgotten. You can still see Hebronites with blue eyes and blond hair who are no doubt the descendants of the crusaders. You can still see families in Palestine with foreign family names like Douglas and Sahyouni (Zion), as well as common Arabic family names reflecting national origin such as Masri (Egyptian), Kurdi (Kurdish), Othmani (Ottoman), Yemeni, Moghrabi (Moroccan), Farisi (Persian), and Saudi.

A while back, I found myself defending a claim made by a fellow Christian Palestinian living in the US. Amer Zahr is an American Palestinian comedian who often produces highly provocative videos. He made a great video stressing that Jesus was Palestinian, a description that angered many who insisted that he was Jewish. Of course, none of those who were angry at the title, "Jesus is Palestinian," had seen the video, in which Amer goes deep into the multi layers of the people of Palestine. And yes, he has no problem in talking about the faith of Jesus of Galilee.

I defended Amer on X (Twitter) and other interactive social media platforms, arguing, as he did, that Jesus was both Jewish in terms of his religion at the time, but he was also Palestinian because he lived in Palestine.

Palestinians have suffered from continuous occupation, foreign rule, and colonial settlement powers trying to control and lay roots in our land only to be defeated. In the second half of the second millennium, the Turkish Ottomans ruled Palestine as part of their regional Ottoman Empire that spanned the entire east Mediterranean region. The 400 years of Ottoman rule left Palestine and the region in bad shape due to their lack of effort, if not total neglect, in developing education, health, and other basic public service institutions.

While looking at the roots of the people of all faiths and ethnicities that lived in Palestine, namely the land between the River and the Sea, is necessary, it is perhaps more helpful to focus on the 20th century, which one can argue had set the foundational background for the current Palestinian Arab vs. Israeli Jew conflict that we have been witnessing for decades.

Twentieth Century

Before diving into the 20th century, let me point out two important indisputable facts that occurred a century earlier.

One: Jews in Europe and North Africa had lived in peace and comradeship and protected each other from racist Europeans.

Two: The ideology of the current conflict was born in the 19th century by Jewish Europeans who were rightly upset with the racism and the anti-Jewish stereotyping that existed in Europe. Theodor Herzl and Vladimir Jabotinsky, both secular European Jews, gave birth to the Zionist movement, whose entire purpose was the creation of a Jewish state as a response to the discrimination that Jews were experiencing in Europe. Naturally, the biggest problem of Zionism is that it was born on the lie that Palestine was "a land without people for a people without land." We will not delve into the peoplehood of Palestinians – many learned authors have written plenty on this issue – however, we will largely deal with the historic and current realities in Palestine as they occurred in the 20th century and first quarter of the 21st century.

At the turn of the 20th century, the Ottoman Empire was collapsing, and Arab nationalism was growing. When we were growing up, our parents reconfirmed what we were always taught in school: that Palestine and the Arab world were kept ignorant, uneducated, and backward for centuries by the Ottomans. It was often referred to as the 400 years of ignorance. With its capital in Constantinople (modern-day Istanbul) controlling a sizable portion of the Mediterranean Basin, the Ottoman Empire was at the center of interactions between the Middle East and Europe for centuries.

Some of the stories we heard from our parents and grandparents focused on World War I and the Turkish preparation for the war by means of forced conscription of men from all the countries under Ottoman control. Stories about falsifying birth certificates to avoid conscription or running away as they were recruited for the war dominate early lure in our and many other families.

Sick and tired of the Ottomans, Arabs aligned themselves with the British with the hope that they would be free once the war was over. Arab leaders prepared themselves for independence post-World War I and made connections with the Brits to ensure that once the Ottomans were defeated, the Arab people who were living under Ottoman rule would be liberated. Some of this historic episode was depicted in the Hollywood film *Lawrence of Arabia*, but, in fact, the Arab position of allying with the British was a strategic one that was well documented in what is often referred to as the Hussein-McMahon Correspondence.

These were a series of letters that were exchanged in 1915-1916 during World War I between Hussein ibn Ali, emir (Sharif) of Mecca, and Sir Henry McMahon, the British high commissioner in Egypt, in which the Government of the United Kingdom agreed to recognize Arab independence in a large region after the war in exchange for the Sharif of Mecca launching the Arab Revolt against the Ottoman Empire. Those promises in the correspondence, however, were almost simultaneously contradicted with opposing pledges made to Jewish Zionists in Britain.

Growing up in Jerusalem in the second half of the 20th century, November 2nd was an infamous date most of us could never forget. It was the date when Arthur Balfour, the British foreign secretary in 1917, signed away our country to a Jewish businessman. The entire transaction was reduced into a mere 100-word letter from Balfour to Lionel Walter Rothschild, a wealthy Zionist leader of the British Jewish community.

The letter, which was kept secret for a while, became the Balfour Declaration and was construed as a British public pledge declaring its aim to establish "a national home for the Jewish people" in Palestine. After World War I ended with the defeat of the Ottomans, British General Edmund Allenby rode into Jerusalem to begin a period of British mandatory rule that would last until 15 May 1948.

Most Palestinians don't know the British general's first name, but since he came from the East Bank of Jordan via a small wooden bridge over the Jordan River, his last name became associated with the Bridge. If you want to use one word to make the blood of modern Palestinians boil, just mention the Allenby Bridge. Israel, which occupied the West Bank in June 1967, made the Allenby Bridge the only port for entry and exit to and from Jordan and through Jordan to the rest of the world. For decades, this bridge has and continues to be the single most excruciating border crossing that individuals and families cringe at when remembering the hours of waiting in the hot Jordan Valley heat, the humiliating body search, and the intensive intelligence questioning.

Naturally, all that is for those who grind their teeth in the hope of returning home, entering to see loved ones, or even visiting holy places.

Imagine the tens of thousands over the years who go through all this suffering, only to be denied entry by an Israeli security official, always without explanation and sometimes over a silly answer that might reveal that you believe Palestinians should be free from occupation.

This singular crossing point is not open 24 hours a day and Palestinians are not allowed to use their own cars to cross this bridge, even though it is the only passage for millions of Palestinians. Anyone wishing a fast crossing has to pay an exorbitant $100 a person to make the three-kilometer crossing and avoid the long hours of waiting in overcrowded buses.

The Jordanians called the crossing point the King Hussein Bridge, and although Israel has officially accepted that name of the late Jordanian leader who made peace with Israel, most Israelis and others still refer to this notorious spot as the Allenby Bridge. I have literally wasted months of my life waiting in line, arguing with Israeli security officials, and feeling frustrated every time I crossed this bridge. I crossed this bridge so many times that my staff in Ramallah once gave me a certificate as the Bridge expert. I could easily author an entire book about this bridge, but I am sure it would not be a pleasant read.

General Allenby is also remembered for a symbolic gesture during his entry into Jerusalem. Unlike the German Emperor Kaiser Wilhelm II, who, during his 1898 visit, insisted on riding his horse into the Old City through the Jaffa Gate, Allenby chose a humbler approach. Kaiser Wilhelm, a tall man fond of grand displays, found the gate not high enough for him and his favorite horse. In response, he ensured the Ottomans dismantled part of the ancient wall where the gate stood to allow for his unhindered entrance.

In contrast, the victorious British general dismounted and walked into the holy city on foot as a sign of respect and humility. He later exited through Jaffa Gate, this time on horseback. Today, anyone passing through Jaffa Gate can still see the break in the historic wall made for the Kaiser's entrance.

Though the original gate structure is gone, the opening remains known as Jaffa Gate.

However, unlike the rest of the post-war mandates, the main goal of the British Mandate in Palestine was to create the conditions for the establishment of a Jewish "national home" – where Jews constituted less than 10 percent of the population at the time.

Upon the start of the mandate, the British began to facilitate the immigration of European Jews to Palestine. Between 1922 and 1935, the Jewish population jumped from 9 percent to nearly 27 percent of the total population.

Though the Balfour Declaration included the caveat that "nothing shall be done which may prejudice the civil and religious rights of existing non-Jewish communities in Palestine," the British Mandate was set up in a way to equip Jews with the tools to establish self-rule at the expense of the Palestinian Arabs.

Edward Said, the brilliant Palestinian scholar, summarized the Balfour Declaration as having been "made by a European power ... about a non-European territory ... in a flat disregard of both the presence and wishes of the native majority resident in that territory."

In essence, the Balfour Declaration promised Jews a land where the natives made up more than 90 percent of the population.

The revelation of both the Hussein-McMahon letters and the Balfour Declaration shamefully exposes the fact that the Brits simply double crossed the Arabs by simultaneously promising Palestine to the Jews.

Post World War I

The period after the end of World War I witnessed a robust emigration of Jews to Palestine with the help, or at times a blind eye, of the British mandatory powers. Protests calling for a halt or the need to organize the unregulated emigration of Jews to Palestine failed in part by the Jewish terror groups, mainly the Irgun, headed by Menahem Begin, who later became Israel's prime minister. Let me here reference Encyclopedia Britannica, which describes

Irgun as a "Jewish right-wing underground movement in Palestine, founded in 1931. At first supported by many nonsocialist Zionist parties, in opposition to the Haganah, it became in 1936 an instrument of the Revisionist Party, an extreme nationalist group that had seceded from the World Zionist Organization and whose policies called for the use of force, if necessary, to establish a Jewish state on both sides of the Jordan River."

Irgun committed acts of terrorism and assassination against the British, whom it regarded as illegal occupiers, and it was also violently anti-Arab. Irgun participated in the organization of illegal immigration into Palestine after the publication of the British White Paper on Palestine (1939), which severely limited immigration. Irgun's violent activities led to execution of many of its members by the British; in retaliation, Irgun executed British army hostages.

However, the biggest and most organized, trained, and equipped Jewish underground group was the Haganah, which later became the nucleus of the Israeli army.

World War II and the uptick in anti-Jewish sentiments in Europe, followed by the horrific holocaust, escalated emigration to Palestine as well as world sympathy for the Jews that was exemplified in the swift and broad recognition by world powers, beginning with the US and the Soviet Union, of the nascent state of Israel.

Balfour to Nakba

I was asked by editors of *The Cairo Review of Global Affairs*, the American University in Cairo's quarterly journal, to read and comment on an important book by Palestinian academic Rashid Khalidi, the Edward Said Chair at Columbia University in New York, entitled *The Hundred Years' War: A History of Settler Colonialism and Resistance, 1917-2017*.

In his book, Khalidi breaks the hundred years of war on Palestine into six periods. He describes the Balfour Declaration and all the British bias in favor of Jewish Zionists that followed, especially between 1917 and 1939, as the first declaration of war on Palestine. He shows with skill and documentation the simple fact that the great colonial power at the time, Great Britain, not only acquiesced with Jewish Zionists, but also went overboard in denying the existence of the Palestinian people and Palestinian nationalism.

Khalidi argues that while settler colonialism was ending in the middle of the 20th century, it was just beginning in Palestine.

My personal knowledge of this period comes from my dad, George Kuttab, who often talked about the nonviolent resistance of Palestinian Arabs in the 1930s, which culminated in a six-month general strike from April to October 1936. That strike produced the 1939 British White Paper that would have brought better results had it not been for the division among Palestinian leaders. We were often told, as we grew up, about the famous British policy of divide and rule.

They appeared to have perfected the system on us by dividing Palestinian families in Jerusalem between the Husseinis and the Nashashibis and successfully driving a wedge between Palestinian fellaheen (peasants) and city dwellers. Again, artificial divisions, but the result weakened Palestinian unity and led to the failure of reaching a solution that would preserve Palestine.

Sadly, what happened at the time has happened on many occasions since with a lot of bravado talk and little honest analysis, proper planning, and efficient execution of plans. Slogans were easy to come by, but anyone trying to produce a realistic plan that would preserve Palestinian presence was often accused of treason or abandonment of the cause.

The entire Palestinian movement went for all and lost all. On the other hand, the Zionists pocketed every single small gain they could grab and built on it with proper planning and execution, and naturally with a lot of help from abroad, while Palestinians were fooled by sweet talk and no action.

The importance of this period is truly relevant to our situation today. It brings into question the Palestinian leaders' failure to produce results with nonviolent action, partly due to the divisions within Palestine and the inability to sustain the protests, thanks to the intervention of outside parties as well as the brutality of the British mandatory powers.

During the second part of this revolt, a leader by the name of Izzedin al-Qassam emerged, and his killing triggered a more violent protest that was put down even more harshly by the British.

Izzedin al-Qassam, a Syrian Islamic preacher, immigrated to Palestine in 1920, where he became a Muslim waqf (religious endowment) official and grew incensed at the plight of Palestinian Arab peasants.

He advocated a moral, political, and military jihad as the solution to end British rule and Zionist aspirations in Palestine.

Al-Qassam has become a symbol for current Palestinian resistance. The Islamic Resistance Movement, Hamas, has called its military wing the Izzedin al-Qassam Brigades, whose current leader Yahya Sinwar led the 7 October cross border attack against Israel and has conducted the resistance to the Israeli genocidal war against Palestinians in Gaza.

Sinwar was killed a little over one year later, in October 2024, in a battle in Rafah, debunking the Israeli portrayal of hiding in tunnels and surrounding himself with Israeli hostages.

Interestingly, the leader of the Fatah Tanzim (movement) in the West Bank, Marwan Barghouti, named his oldest son Qassam in a similar tribute to the armed resistance leader who fought the Zionists in the 1930s.

Nakba of 1947-1948

While the British were busy putting down the Palestinian armed resistance, the Zionists were building up their own underground forces. World War II put a temporary halt in the situation in Palestine, only to come back with a vengeance following the end of the war, the victory of the allies, and the discovery of the appalling holocaust that had befallen millions of Jews as well as others. The combined nature of the rise of antisemitism in Europe, official Christian Europeans acquiescence to the discrimination and annihilation against Jews, and sympathy for Jews led to a huge increase in emigration to Palestine and an escalation of the underground attacks against the British mandatory police.

The Jewish underground movements like Irgun, whose leader Menahem Begin was charged with terrorism by the British but was never caught, hastened the British exit. My dad often told us the story of how Begin and his men loaded milk containers with explosives on 22 June 1946 and drove them to the basement of the King David Hotel in Jerusalem, which was then used as the headquarters of the British mandatory powers, and blew it up, killing British mandatory leaders and staff. Ninety-one people were killed, including 21 first-rank government officials, 49 second-rank clerks, 13 soldiers, three police officers, and five bystanders. By nationality, the dead were 41 Arabs, 28 British citizens, 17 Jews, two Armenians, one Russian, one Greek, and one Egyptian. Forty-nine people were injured.

UN General Assembly Resolution 181 dividing Palestine into a Jewish and an Arab state, with Jerusalem and Jaffa being international cities, was passed in 1947, partly due to extortion and extraordinary pressure on Latin American countries. Zionists in Tel Aviv celebrated at the time and continued their pressure on the British. In many debates and discussions around the world, I have often been confronted with the question of why the Palestinians rejected the Partition Plan. I had once asked my dad that question and he explained to me that Palestinian Arabs were much of the population and owned the majority of the land of Palestine, yet the plan offered by the UN gave the minority population, the Jews, the majority of the land.

The estimates of the British mandatory powers in 1945 put the total area of land owned by Jews at 1.5 million dunams, compared to about 13 million dunams owned by Arabs in Palestine. As for the population and despite the large number of illegal immigrants flooding to Palestine, Jews accounted for no more than one third of the total population of Palestine at the time of the Partition Plan. So, my dad was correct in that the UN awarded the minority population that owned a small portion of Palestinian land most of the land to set up their own state on it. Naturally, Jewish Zionists in Tel Aviv celebrated, yet they continued their strategic military actions aimed at forcing the British to leave.

The increased Jewish underground attacks appeared to speed up the exit of the Brits from Palestine.

The well organized and armed Zionists, with some having been trained by the allies, began a campaign of terror aimed at emptying as many Palestinians as possible to make room for their new state that was yet to be declared. They committed many massacres, some like the Deir Yassin massacre west of Jerusalem on 9 April 1948, a day after the Palestinian leader Abdel Qader al-Husseini, who led the sparsely armed Palestinian resistance forces, was killed in battle. Jewish terrorists killed 200 Palestinian civilians in a massacre that prompted even more families to leave their homes and flee for their lives.

Years later as I was working as a journalist in Jerusalem, Miriam, our neighbor in Sheikh Jarrah, told us part of the story of the massacre. She was the only member of her family who survived the mass killings of civilians in Deir Yassin. According to her account, many of the town's men who were supposed to be on guard in the area decided to attend the funeral of the Palestinian leader in Jerusalem, leaving their village sparsely guarded and the women and children vulnerable. This allowed the Zionists to kill the women and children of the village with ease and take over the town in the strategically elevated location.

Danger also nearly hit other friends of our family. Reverend Ibrahim Oweis, a Syrian Christian who was appointed as pastor of the Christian and Missionary Alliance Church in the old city of Jerusalem, was living in the largely Christian Qatamon area in Jerusalem when Jewish terrorists attacked the nearby Semiramis Hotel.

On the night of 5-6 January 1948, the Jewish Haganah, at the time under the leadership of who would become Israel's first prime minister David Ben-Gurion, bombed the hotel, killing no less than 24 civilians, including at least one child. Seven members of the Abou Souan family, Hubert Lorenzo, the 23-year-old son of the hotel proprietor, and Spanish vice-consul Manuel Allende

Salazar were among those killed in the attack.

The explosion shook Reverend Oweis's house, but the family was fortunately saved. In later years during a visit to Canada, I met with Paul Oweis, the dentist son of the pastor who showed me photos of the blown-up hotel and told me the story firsthand. Paul's father was my wife Salam Madanat's late uncle. Salam's father, Reverend Odeh Madanat, had taken over running the same church and later marrying Paul's aunt Maha Oweis.

The violence worked and the British mandatory powers announced that they would leave Palestine on 15 May 1948. This launched another violent period that Palestinians call the *Nakba*, the catastrophe which included a series of terrorist massacres that forced 750,000 Palestinians to leave their towns and homes with a few belongings and armed with the hope that they would return as soon as the hostilities ended. They have yet to return.

The catastrophe, of course, affected our family. My dad succeeded in leaving their Musrara home early in 1948 to take a job running a Church-owned school in Zarqa in the East Bank of the Jordan River. Dad took his mother and left older brother Qustandi to watch over their home. But tragedy would soon hit the Kuttab clan when my aunt Hoda's husband, Elias Awad, who lived near my dad's family home in Musrara, was killed in 1948 by a Jewish sharpshooter stationed in the Notre Dame Hotel area just outside the New Gate.

His murder left Aunt Hoda a widow with seven children; the youngest was one-year-old Alex. My uncle Qustandi, realizing the danger was extremely near, locked up the house, making sure he turned the key twice, as he told my dad upon arriving in Zarqa. Uncle Qustandi would become an officially registered refugee with a card from UNRWA, the UN Relief and Works Agency for Palestine Refugees, which ensured he and his family would get the rations that the UN would provide until their return home.

Our uncle Qustandi lived in Bethlehem and used his *cart al wakaleh* (the UNRWA card) to get basic subsistence for years. His oldest son, Maurice, studied medicine at the prestigious American University of Beirut and ended up living and working in the US. The family followed Maurice to the state of Tennessee where they lived. My uncle and his wife passed away as did Maurice, but his children Elias, Munira, and Gloria and their kids, like millions of descendants of Palestinian refugees in the diaspora, are still living in the United States.

Chapter Three

Nakba to Naksa 1948-1967 and beyond

Israeli lust for land without the people despite claims of peace

Although Jewish Zionists welcomed the 1947 Partition Plan that divided historic Palestine into a Jewish and an Arab state, the new state of Israel and its supporters pocketed whatever the United Nations had gifted them and proceeded to capture the rest of the areas between the sea and the river.

When the dust of the 1948 war settled and the 1949 Armistice Agreement was reached, it became clear that the newly announced state of Israel was already larger than the country that the UN had carved out for them. Jaffa, which was supposed to be an international enclave, was swallowed up by the state of Israel. Jerusalem was divided into west Jerusalem in the hands of Israel and was largely ethnically cleansed of its original Palestinian population, while the old city and some of the surrounding areas east of the old city were in Arab hands.

Jordan would take custody of the West Bank and within a few years annex it to the Hashemite Kingdom of Jordan in an act that was superficially supported by Palestinian signature in a conference of some tribal Palestinian leaders with allegiance to the Jordanian crown. Gaza became an Egyptian protectorate, and whoever was living in it (almost half were newly arriving refugees) would hold Egyptian travel documents stating that they were Palestinians.

Much has been said and written about this period, but among the most memorable images that have been imprinted in many Palestinian minds have been the artworks of Ismail Shamout, especially one painting that the artist titled *Where To?* The image depicts a father (or perhaps a grandfather) carrying one child on his shoulder and holding the hand of another while gripping a cane in the other hand.

A third boy is walking right behind him. Unlike the mercy-seeking images of victims in refugee camps, this intense painting of a dignified Palestinian man, despite his modest clothes, exhausted looking children, and being kicked out of his homeland in 1948, became the dominant image of the Palestinian national movement that would emerge in the 1960s and ignite Palestinian nationalism.

Iqrit and Biram

While Palestinians and Palestinian refugees were generally ignored after the Nakba, a further sub-Palestinian community was even more disregarded. Many Palestinian Christians from Jaffa, Haifa, Lydda, Ramleh, and what later became known as West Jerusalem left under the fire of the Israeli underground forces and their fear-induced massacres, especially in Deir Yasin. But a small Palestinian Christian community survived in the Nazareth and Galilee areas, often in towns and villages with strong church leaderships. However, the residents of two Palestinian Christian villages are further victims of the Zionist policy of attempting to empty the land from its original inhabitants.

Few people around the world have heard the names Iqrit and Biram. But for Palestinian citizens of Israel, especially those living in the Galilee, the story of Iqrit and Biram are well known. I stumbled on this story in the 1980s when I met the Mansour family in Nazareth and their journalist patriarch Atallah Mansour. I had met Botrus, his oldest son who was studying law in Jerusalem's Hebrew University, and I heard about these two towns when I visited the family in Nazareth. Since the 7 October events in Gaza and the constant Israeli efforts to "convince" Palestinians to temporarily leave Gaza for Sinai "for their own safety," I have tried to remind people of what happened more than 75 years earlier.

Six months after the state of Israel was established, some military skirmishes would break out between combatants from South Lebanon and the newly established Israeli army. Local leaders of the residents of the two predominantly Palestinian Christian villages of Iqrit and Biram, who had become citizens of the state that now ruled over them, were asked politely to leave their villages. The request was made in November 1948, about five months after the war had ended. The local leaders were told they could return "within two weeks" or as soon as the dangers no longer existed.

They left voluntarily believing in the sincerity of the new rulers who had created what was said to be an enlightened state that lived by the rule of law. From that day until today (November 2024), the state of Israel has never allowed them to return, not that they didn't try and are still trying. Their efforts have always been nonviolent, as Father Elias Chacour explained so vividly in his best-selling book *Blood Brothers*.

At one point in the winter of 1950, it appeared that the legal efforts would allow their return. The Israeli High Court sided with the village residents and set a date for their return on 25 December 1950. But on Christmas Eve of that year, the night before that holy Christian day celebrating the birth of Christ, Israeli Air Force fighters were dispatched to bomb all the homes in the two villages except the two churches – a Maronite Church in Iqrit and a Melkite Catholic Church in Biram. Nonviolent efforts to return have continued for decades, and at one time, the Likud party leader

Menachem Begin had promised the villagers that if he became prime minister, he would ensure their return. He became as such, but they never were allowed to return, allegedly for fear that if they returned, other Palestinians disposed of during the 1948 War – whether living outside Israel or inside – would follow the precedent and request their right to return. While Israel, which had become a recognized UN state in 1950, had pledged to honor UN Resolution 194 calling for the return *and* compensation of Palestinian refugees, reneged on its word and continued to reject their right of return.

Although the new Israeli leaders were not willing to honor the right of the indigenous Palestinians to return, one of the earliest of these laws was the 1950 Law of Return, which enshrined the right of Jews to come to Israel, settle, and automatically receive citizenship. I once met a Canadian NGO activist of Middle Eastern origin who had a Jewish mother and a Palestinian father. He jokingly told me that he may be the only person in the world who enjoys both the 194 UN right of return (as guaranteed to his Palestinian father and his father's descendants) and the Israeli Law of Return that guarantees the return of any person on the planet that had at least a Jewish mother. He didn't request either right, he insisted to me.

In the following decades, the Palestinian Christians who remained within the Israel-claimed territory faced the same apartheid regime that Palestinian Muslims did. They have been subjected to about 65 racist laws that deprive them of the same rights as Jewish citizens of Israel, according to research done by the Haifa-based Adalah NGO.

The policy of discrimination continues in the state of Israel against its citizens and in a much more brutal apartheid way in the occupied territories. The Israeli Knesset passed the Nation State Bill in 2018, which formally declares Israel as the nation-state of the Jewish people, thus further solidifying the legal iteration of Jewish supremacy. This emboldened the extremist elements within Israeli society even more and encouraged the heightening of anti-Palestinian violence.

Meanwhile, Israeli lust for Palestinian land became evident within a few years at a regional level. In October 1956, Israel joined the French and British invasion of Egypt under the pretext of reversing the nationalization of the Suez Canal. The war, which the Arabs call the Tripartite Aggression, ended abruptly with the intervention of the US president at the time, Dwight Eisenhower. The retreating Israelis, however, did not return to the 1949 Armistice Agreement lines, but took over a sliver of Gaza land that became known as the Gaza envelope area. Unlike most countries that went to great lengths to keep their citizens safe, Israel pushed its citizens as close as possible to the borders with Gaza on the newly stolen lands of the Gaza Strip. Ironically, this area would become the target of Hamas fighters on 7 October 2023 as they tried to break out of a 16-year siege on Gaza that followed the Islamist's win in the 2006 Palestinian elections and the withdrawal of Palestinian national forces loyal to President Mahmoud Abbas in Ramallah.

The 1967 Naksa

Israeli hunger for Palestinian land took a major step on 5 June 1967 when Israel initiated a multi-country war on Egypt, Jordan, and Syria. In a blitz military operation, Israel captured the entire Gaza Strip, the West Bank, the Sinai Peninsula including the eastern bank of the Suez Canal, and the Syrian Golan Heights.

The justification for the Israeli attack was two-fold. This was a pre-emptive strike against Egypt that had ordered the closure of the Strait of Hormuz, effectively causing a kind of maritime siege on Israel's Red Sea port of Eilat, coupled with the boisterous rhetoric of Egyptian President Gamal Abdel Nasser and his propagandists on Sawt al-Arab (Voice of the Arabs) Radio.

Politically, Israel was quick to claim that they would happily relinquish the Palestinian territories, except for East Jerusalem which it had annexed within weeks of the 5 June war and had tripled its size.

Stunned by the June defeat they called the *Naksa* (setback), Arab leaders met in the Sudanese capital Khartoum and declared that they have no plans to negotiate or make peace with Israel. They issued what has become the infamous three No's: No negotiations, no recognition, and no peace with Israel.

Those three Arab No's would become the focus of the Israeli propaganda machine, which would continue for decades as the narrative that peace and withdrawal from occupied Palestinian lands were not possible because the other side did not want peace.

UN Security Council Resolution 242 was carefully crafted, requiring the officially binding version to call for Israeli withdrawal from "lands occupied in the recent conflict" rather than *"all" or "the* lands occupied," giving Israel itself a green light to exclude Jerusalem from any talks. The resolution also called on Arabs to resolve the conflict peacefully, and therefore, Israel felt no obligation to give up Palestinian land so long as the Arabs were rejecting peace as referenced by the resolutions of the Khartoum Arab League Summit of September 1967.

The Israeli rejection of peace, in action but not in words, was not limited to its unilateral annexation of East Jerusalem. Within a few years was the beginning of an illegal Jewish settlement enterprise that violated the Fourth Geneva Convention, which considered the movement of people from an occupying power to the occupied territories to be a war crime.

Occupied vs. disputed territories

Israel in all its branches, including the judiciary, refused to deal with the Palestinian territories captured during the June 1967 war as occupied. Instead, they claimed those territories to be disputed because when they were taken, they were not Palestinian lands, and that Jordan, which was occupying the West Bank, had not obtained the recognition of its annexation of the area except from Britain and Pakistan. This meant, in Israeli eyes, that these territories were disputed. While the Israelis kept the name of Gaza for Palestine's southern strip, they decided to call the West Bank by the Hebrew term Judea and Samaria, the first step in what would become a decades-long debate as to whose land this belonged, even though international law was very clear. Some of the liberal Israelis who didn't want to concede the West Bank to be part of a Palestinian state but also were opposed to religious Jewish nationalism decided to create their term, *Shtakhim,* which means "territories;" thus, leaving the adjective as to whether this was occupied or disputed up for grabs.

But for the international community, and especially the UNSC, there was no question that these are occupied territories and that in the post-World War II global view, countries are no longer allowed to settle their land disputes in this manner. The preamble of UNSC Resolution 242 addressed this issue clearly by stating: "Emphasizing the inadmissibility of the acquisition of territory by war and the need to work for a just and lasting peace in which every State in the area can live in security."

As a result of the powerful Israeli hasbara (roughly translated explaining but in reality, a form of Israeli propaganda), there is always an effort to keep the issue from being firmly resolved. When Palestinians appealed to the International Court of Justice for an advisory opinion on the legality of the Israeli wall deep in Palestinian territory, Israel tried its best to sow doubt about the nature of the Palestinian territories. In the end, it failed to sway the court from certifying that the areas occupied in 1967 were occupied territories. A similar Israeli effort was made when the Palestinian Football Association complained to FIFA, the International Football Federation, that six Israeli settlement-based football clubs in the West Bank were breaking the FIFA bylaws by playing in Palestinian territories outside the Palestinian Federation, Israel kept arguing that the West Bank was a disputed territory.

Again, the UN and other international bodies were asked to adjudicate the legal issue of the status of the Palestinian territories.

Even when the relevant UN agencies answered clearly that it occupied Palestinian territories, Israel continued to violate the FIFA bylaws, and the international organizations buried the Palestinian complaint in committees and bureaucracies to this day. Meanwhile, the settlement clubs have not been barred from playing in the Israeli league or internationally.

The discussion, however, especially after the war on Gaza raged, resulted in the withdrawal of PUMA, the giant international sports company, from sponsoring the Israeli clubs.

Jewish settlements

Perhaps the biggest obstacle to the creation of an independent Palestinian state in 2024 is the existence of illegal Jewish Israelis who have left the internationally recognized state of Israel within the boundaries of the pre-June 1967 war and decided to move into the occupied territories. Their aim was clear in their belief that they are the descendants of Jews returning to their land after thousands of years. It made little difference that Palestinian Arabs have been living on this land for centuries and that they had inhabited the land from time immemorial as documented in the Holy Bible, which refers to Arabs both in the Old and New Testaments. Perhaps the most important reference is that when the Apostle Peter was divinely empowered to speak to thousands on the day of Pentecost, one of the languages he spoke was Arabic, as mentioned in the book of Acts 2:11.

A Jewish couple by the name of Moshe and Miriam Levinger, along with a few other

Israelis, checked into a Hebron hotel on 4 April 1968 pretending to be Swiss tourists. The next day, they declare that they are not leaving the city, setting off a debate about Jewish efforts to repopulate the Palestinian Arab city. Eventually, Israel decides to let the group live at an adjacent Israeli army base, which becomes the community of Kiryat Arba. Now the Jewish settlement of Kiryat Arba has a population of nearly 7,500 Israeli citizens.

They are entitled to political and civil rights in Israel both in terms of elections and receiving Israeli social support, such as free medical insurance and other social benefits, as well as freedom of movement through Palestinian areas to Israel and back to Hebron, which the indigenous Palestinian population doesn't have, of course.

They also receive larger amounts of water than the Palestinian population at subsidized rates. The Jewish settler population grew in Hebron over the years, often moving into Israeli army locations and denying local Palestinians access to their own streets and shops. Al- Shuhada Street, one of the biggest central town market streets, is a good case in point as a no-go zone for Palestinians.

The tensions between the heavily armed settlers and their Israeli army protectors have reached a height that international organizations, like the Christian Peacemaker teams, would bring volunteers from around the world with the simple job of escorting Palestinian children in Hebron on their way to school and back past the newly established homes.

Levinger's wife, Miriam, led the resettlement of the Old Jewish Quarter in Hebron in 1979 when she and nine other women and 40 children sneaked into the Beit Hadassah clinic and made it their home.

After a Palestinian attack in front of the building killed six yeshiva students in 1980, Prime Minister Begin's government allowed the expansion of Jewish settlement in the city.

Hebron was the scene of one of the worst incidents of Jewish terrorism against Palestinians on 25 February 1994, when Baruch Goldstein, a doctor who was dressed in army fatigues, killed 29 Muslim worshippers at the Al-Ibrahimi Mosque (Tomb of the Patriarchs) and wounded 125 others while they were literally kneeling during dawn prayers. Goldstein was eventually killed with a fire extinguisher by the surviving Palestinians, although no one knows exactly who killed him since the issue was kept a secret. His supporters have built a shrine for Goldstein in Hebron.

The incident took place during a sensitive period of Yitzhak Rabin's reign and less than a year after the Memorandum of Understanding and mutual recognitions were exchanged and signed by the PLO's Mahmoud Abbas and Israel's Shimon Peres in the presence of PLO leader Yasser Arafat, Rabin, and US President Bill Clinton.

The pressure on Rabin yielded the permission for a Temporary International Presence in Hebron, TIPH, a sort of unarmed international police protection made up of mostly civilian personnel from Scandinavian countries. The TIPH, however, was terminated and expelled by Israeli Prime Minister Benjamin Netanyahu in 2019, ending its 20-year mandate and presence in Hebron.

Elon Moreh and Har Homa

When Begin, the Likud party founder and leader who led the Irgun underground, became Israel's prime minister, a major battle ensued over the effort to settle in the largely Palestinian populated Nablus governorate in the West Bank. Elon Moreh was a Jewish Orthodox settlement that rightfully triggered much anger and protests, but Arab countries, divided after the visit of Egyptian President Anwar Sadat and his speech at the Israeli Knesset in November 1977, had little clout on Israel or the US to pressure Israel.

The success of Elon Moreh, including the shameful approval by the Israeli High Court for its construction, paved the way for the building of 49 similar settlements over the years. Some settlements like Ariel became a city with a university and a direct highway to Israel while barring Palestinians from a wide swath of land around it from building and even sometimes farming their own privately owned lands.

Another Jewish settlement built in the area between Jerusalem and Bethlehem also caused much anger, protests, and even international opposition, but has still survived. Har Homa was built on privately owned land of Palestinians from Beit Sahour in Jabal Abu Ghnaim in 1991 at the height of the Palestinian intifada (uprising). Again, both Palestinian and international efforts failed to stop this huge settlement that, based on 2013 estimates, housed more than 25,000 Jewish Israelis living on Palestinian lands.

Jerusalem and the wall

The biggest settler activity took place in the Jerusalem area, which the Israelis unilaterally annexed and therefore, pay little attention to the international outcry over their activities. Huge city-like settlements were built largely on confiscated Palestinian land as if it was all Jewish land and housing units owned by the Jewish people for eternity. Ironically, Israel and its municipality and regional council have yet to permit the creation of a city zoning plan for East Jerusalem, effectively curtailing the possibility of Palestinians to build homes, especially for young couples. The high cost of apartments in East Jerusalem skyrocketed as the demand far exceeded the supply of homes available to potential buyers. Some Palestinians, most of them citizens of Israel, bought apartments in essentially non-ideological settlements that were built in East Jerusalem because they were available at much more reasonable prices.

The housing problems in East Jerusalem were somewhat resolved when Israel erected an eight-meter-high wall inside East Jerusalem, leaving large portions of the predominantly Palestinian city beyond the wall.

Although still technically Jerusalem, neighborhoods like Kufr Aqab, Samir Amis, and others witnessed the unregulated building boom that included high-rise buildings, which Jerusalem residents could afford to own or rent yet still be considered Jerusalemites. By doing that, they are able to continue to safeguard their residency in the city while living in a dump largely ignored by the Israeli municipality.

Of all the population in the area, Palestinians living in East Jerusalem have been the most consistent municipal taxpayers. The city property tax known as "Arnona" has become the most important document that shows that the person paying it lives in Jerusalem and therefore his or her residency is not revoked like what happened to nearly 20,000 Palestinian Jerusalemites over the years. Israel has never respected the 2004 International Court of Justice decision, taken in a 14-1 vote (opposed was an American judge), rendering the wall as "illegal" and calling on the Israeli government to dismantle it.

Palestinian reaction

In the first years of the occupation, the Jordan option was the Israeli favorite. Some Palestinian dignitaries including mayors went along with this option and some Jordanian officials were also reluctant to give up their role. But with the rise of the PLO, in large part after Jordanian soldiers and Palestinian fedayeen defeated and pushed back the Israeli raiding forces from the East Bank Jordanian town of Karameh, the Jordanian option became irrelevant because the majority of Palestinians favored the PLO. In the 1974 Arab summit in the Moroccan capital of Rabat, Jordan's King Hussein gave up his kingdom's role and the PLO was declared the sole legitimate representative of the Palestinian people. Arafat, the chairman of the PLO Executive Committee, would soon after go to New York and make his famous speech at the UN General Assembly, declaring: "Today I have come bearing an olive branch and a freedom-fighter's gun. Do not let the olive tree branch fall from my hand. I repeat, do not let the olive tree branch fall from my hand."

While the PLO was making headway in Arab and international circles, Palestinians under occupation were caught in a catch-22 situation. If they don't act against occupation, the occupiers are able to claim that theirs is a benevolent occupation; if they act especially violently, they are considered terrorists. Membership or even showing support for the PLO was a crime punishable by prison as was the raising of the Palestinian flag, which Israel repeatedly called the PLO flag, even though it had existed since the 1920s, while the PLO was established in the 1960s.

The emphasis by Palestinians was focused on local municipal elections that brought about a crew of pro-PLO Palestinian nationalists in the 1980s. Jewish settlers, worried about this development, carried out assassination attempts targeting three of those leaders by planting bombs in their cars. Nablus's popular Mayor Bassam Shakaa lost both legs and Ramallah's Karim Khalaf lost one leg. At the same time an Israeli army bomb expert lost his eyesight as the booby-trapped car of the mayor blew up in his face.

In the 1980s, I was the managing editor of *Al Fajr* English weekly. As the Israeli claims that Palestinians did not support the PLO, I was able to convince the reporters of the American *Newsday* and Australian *The Age* newspapers to join us in conducting a public opinion poll. Between the three organizations, we raised $6,000 for a wide survey, which came out in strong support of the PLO. Ironically, the American newspaper that partially funded the poll ran a short story about it once the results apparently were not to the liking of its editors and publisher.

Even when leaders like Mubarak Awad advocated for nonviolent protests and boycotts, he was arrested and deported in June 1988 after spending eight months in Israeli jails. The Israeli High Court approved the request for his deportation and denied his birthright in Jerusalem. Yitzhak Shamir, Israel's former head of the Irgun Jewish gang declared terrorists by the British, had become Israeli prime minister approving the deportation of the first East Jerusalem Palestinian.

Six months later, the Palestinian intifada erupted, creating with it a movement of underground leadership that became known as the Unified Leadership of the Intifada, which generally ran as a de-facto secret leadership mirroring the various factions of the PLO, but with much more knowledge of what can work in the occupied territories.

The first Palestinian intifada is now looked back at with envy for its moderation and the fact that it continued as an unarmed popular resistance movement. But despite the people power that it represented and some of its small breakthroughs, it failed to bring about an end to the Israeli occupation. The ultimate equation of Israeli supremacy and control would continue for decades, despite the fact that Palestinians have shown that they will not accept to live forever under occupation and that international law was clear about the inalienable rights of people, including the Palestinians, to full and genuine independence.

Chapter Four

The international position vis-à-vis the realization of Palestine

For years, Palestinian leaders were hung up on the wording of UN Security Council Resolution 242. The carefully worded resolution failed to speak about Palestinians, didn't order Israel to withdraw from *all* the occupied territories, and downplayed the issue of Palestinian refugees. PLO leaders continued to reject UNSC 242 and 338 until the Palestinian intifada was launched in the occupied territories in 1987. I was very busy with my journalism at the time as the Jerusalem-based Palestine reporter for the Nazareth-based *As Senara*. My friend Botrus Mansour's father, Atallah Mansour, a veteran *Haaretz* journalist, was a junior partner in the weekly paper. The main owner and driver of the weekly was Lutfi Mash'our, a firebrand businessman whose main goal was getting ads and coming up with catchy headlines that would attract readers to achieve his ultimate goal of selling ad space.

I had nothing to do with his business and was given space to report on the occupied territories without any restrictions. I trained and hired a few young local journalists, many of whom are now veteran, well respected media professionals. I remember one day when a young man by the name of Taher Shreiteh came to my office in downtown East Jerusalem asking for my help. He was from Gaza and had taken the unusual move of returning home. He wanted to become a journalist and was wondering if I could help him by setting him up with international journalists. Gazan journalists, who have been largely influenced by Egyptians, were fast on words but slow on facts. I was willing to hire him part time, but my first piece of advice to Taher was that he must be extremely careful with information. He needed to double and triple check details before sending them to me. "If someone makes a claim of Israelis killing someone, make sure that he has in fact lost his life and that you can get his or her full name because it will be published; meaning, you better be damn sure it is a fact." I went even further: "If someone tells you so and so was shot, ask them where? If they say in his leg, make sure they are telling you the truth by finding out whether it was the victim's left or right leg."

Taher took my advice to the letter and would soon become the number one freelance fixer for all major newspapers and wires. Reuters was the first to hire him. I had been friends with their bureau chief during my days at *Al Fajr* English weekly, and I had always chided them for not having Palestinian journalists. I would say that "your bureau is full of Israelis or American Jews. Not one even understands Arabic, yet half of your stories are taking place in the occupied territories." He agreed and I suggested Sami Aboudi, a level-headed Palestinian whose family comes from a village near Ramallah. He would work for them for years and move to Dubai to become a regional editor.

They loved Taher. He would get them all kinds of scoops, including an exclusive interview once with the Hamas leader, Sheikh Ahmed Yassin. *The New York Times*, CBS, Japan's

Yomiuri Shimbun, and others would seek his help as their fixer in Gaza. That interview with Yassin almost resulted in Taher being deported along with more than 400 Islamic and Hamas leaders to south Lebanon in 1992. All the editors of the major media outlets he was working for (Reuters, *New York Times*, and the BBC) called Israeli officials and the media spokespersons to inform them that deporting a professional journalist like Taher Shreiteh was wrong.

The second half of the 1980s witnessed a kind of abandonment by Arabs of the Palestinian cause. Egypt's Anwar Sadat had made his separate peace deal with Israel and regained the Sinai Peninsula, while the PLO and other ideological countries like Algeria, Syria, and Libya didn't go along and had forced the move of the Arab League to Tunisia, where the PLO leadership had relocated after leaving Lebanon in 1982 as a result of the continued Israeli war and siege of Beirut, which finally produced a deal that included the safe passage of PLO fighters out of the Lebanese capital.

Khalil al-Wazir, often referred to as Abu Jihad, was responsible for what the Fatah movement called the western front, in reference to the West Bank. He had been very involved with building up pro-PLO civil society organizations, which had also included *Al Fajr* newspaper that I had worked for and had become managing editor before leaving it.

Intifada

In December 1987, an Israeli truck ran over six Palestinians workers, triggering an uprising in Gaza that quickly spread to the West Bank. I had so many contacts at the time with the foreign media that I, like Taher Shreiteh, was often in demand to translate and accompany journalists in Gaza. I was also freelancing with many of the foreign journalists and bureau chiefs of major media outlets in America, Europe, and even Japan and Australia.

When the protests erupted, the word *intifada* began spreading on everyone's tongue. The term also appeared on leaflets whose header stated that they belonged to the PLO-backed group: the Underground Unified National Leadership of the Intifada.

Dan Fisher, then the Jerusalem bureau chief for the *Los Angeles Times*, asked me to translate those leaflets and I explained to him that the word *intifada* means "shaking off," as in the demand for freedom from occupation. Palestinians opposed the occupation, not Israel. Palestinians' aspirations were for an independent state alongside Israel, not instead of Israel.

Initially, the intifada included the methods of resistance practiced by Martin Luther King Jr., Mahatma Gandhi, and Nelson Mandela. My cousin Mubarak Awad was deported by Israeli Prime Minister Yitzhak Shamir for crisscrossing the occupied Palestinian territories and distributing the Arabic translation of Harvard professor Gene Sharp's writings on nonviolence. Mubarak advocated boycotts of Israeli products, work refusals, and building up the Palestinian economy to prepare for independence.

The intifada brought international media attention and more so when Israeli Defense Minister Yitzhak Rabin called on his soldiers to break the bones of Palestinian who threw stones at Israelis. For Palestinians, stones were readily available on all streets and alleys, making Jewish settlers who passed through Palestinian streets to travel between the West Bank and Israel very vulnerable. One day, a CBS crew with a powerful lens was able to capture Israeli soldiers carrying out Rabin's call.

Despite this visual scoop, I had a problem with how western media was operating and I made sure they knew my position. I would often tell them that they hire Israeli camerapersons to shoot Palestinian demonstrators with their cameras during 11 months of the year and then shoot the same Palestinian demonstrators with real M16 rifles during the one-month mandatory army reserve duty they must serve until they are 55 years old. Some major companies like the BBC agreed to add a Palestinian soundman and CBS hired a Palestinian cameraman.

Although I helped Reuters hire a Palestinian in their newsroom and work with Taher in Gaza, as well as the fact that a few television companies had started giving small jobs to Palestinians, still the overwhelming international media was Israeli-staffed.

One day a visitor from New York I had met years earlier stopped by. Ilan Ziv had refused to serve in the Israeli army for conscientious reasons and decided to live in the US. He had been making documentaries around the world and had developed his own theory of using media as a way of capturing what he would call the phenomena of People Power. And the largely non-lethal Palestinian intifada fit that description.

We both agreed that we can't make a documentary film using the existing Israeli crews, especially in major Palestinian cities that had been bustling with anti-Israeli energy. We talked about empowering young Palestinian filmmakers. Material filmed on small new cameras, Super VHS, had become acceptable by major companies and we decided to try and develop a project of documenting life in the occupied territories. Israel was often placing major cities under curfew, which further restricted even non-Israeli international crews. Our idea was to supply four young filmmakers with the new cameras and have them film from inside the crowded Palestinian towns whether under curfew or not. We agreed that we would meet in Jerusalem once a month, pick up whatever they filmed, review it, and give them further instructions. I had become involved with a new company called Al Quds Television Productions (ATP), which became a Tamouz (Ilan's company) and ATP co-production. Ilan succeeded in getting BBC Channel 4 and the Dutch company IKON to fund the production phase. We had Abdel Salam Shehada from Rafah, Suhair Ismail from the village of Khader near Bethlehem, and Nazih Darwazeh from the old city of Nablus. Nazih Darwazeh, who later worked for Associated Press TV, was shot dead by Israeli soldiers in his hometown of Nablus as he was taking footage of Israeli incursion into the city.

Our ATP office in Jerusalem was next to the American Colony Hotel, where many western journalists would stay, and also on the same street as the Orient House, a historic building owned by the Husseini family run by Faisal Husseini, the son of the leader Abdel Qader killed in 1948. Faisal Husseini was a rising star among Palestinians in Jerusalem, along with Sari Nusseibeh, a professor and political strategist. The two made an excellent team with Faisal as the charismatic and popular public leader and Sari as the behind-the-scenes thinker.

Palestinian Declaration of Independence

In the first year of the intifada, an idea was born. Since the protests were always emphasizing that they are against the occupation and not against the state of Israel within its internationally recognized borders, why not turn this into a high-level political decision. The idea was for the PLO to declare a Palestinian state on part of Palestine, more or less in accordance with the often rejected UNSC Resolutions 242 and 338. Early drafts of the declaration were reportedly found in the desks of Husseini, but thanks to the power of the fax machine at the time, there were plenty of copies of those early drafts. Palestinian poet laureate Mahmoud Darwish was said to have been assigned by Yasser Arafat to write up the declaration. I was asked by the Japanese *Yomiuri Shimbun* to accompany their reporter as their fixer/translator to the Algerian capital in November 1988, where the Palestine

National Council was meeting and Arafat was ready to declare a Palestinian state that will live in peace with its neighbors, thus, de facto accepting the previously opposed UNSC resolutions. It was considered a peace gesture that the PLO hoped would open up dialogue between the Palestinian leadership and Washington.

In the occupied territories as our teams were constantly recording life under occupation, the Israelis literally turned off the electricity on 15 November 1988 in order to prevent Palestinians from hearing the declaration of a Palestinian state. That, however, failed to keep Palestinians in the dark about their own future and the declaration idea received overwhelming support.

Arafat made his dramatic speech that recognized the presence of followers of the three monotheistic religions (Jews, Christians, and Muslims) and spoke of the powerful influence of the Palestinian intifada. I felt very humbled by the role, along with Dan Fisher of the *Los Angeles Times*, in promoting the term in 1988 and making *intifada* a household word in America and the English-speaking world.

I was in main hall of Qasr al-Snober (the Pine Palace) when this speech was made, and I specifically recall when the following words were uttered by the Chairman of the PLO:

> "Whereas the Palestinian people reaffirms most definitively its inalienable rights in the land of its patrimony:

> "Now by virtue of natural, historical and legal rights, and the sacrifices of successive generations who gave of themselves in defense of the freedom and independence of their homeland;

> "In pursuance of Resolutions adopted by Arab summit conferences and relying on the authority bestowed by international legitimacy as embodied in the resolutions

of the United Nations Organization since 1947;

"And in exercise by the Palestinian Arab people of its rights to self-determination, political independence and sovereignty over its territory;

"The Palestine National Council, in the name of God, and in the name of the Palestinian Arab people, hereby proclaims the establishment of the State of Palestine on our Palestinian territory with its capital Jerusalem (Al-Quds Ash-Sharif)."

After those words were declared, hundreds of green, red, white, and black balloons representing the colors of the Palestinian flag were released to thunderous clapping and a standing ovation. I would be lying if I said that I didn't feel a wave of Palestinian pride and patriotism wash over me the moment that the leader of the Palestinian people, Yasser Arafat, was declaring Palestinian statehood.

However, it would take some time for the intifada to bear fruit.

In the 1990s and as a result of the intifada, I was working with my colleague George Khleifi to set up the Jerusalem Film Institute, where we invited Palestinian filmmakers to attend as their works were screened for the first time to Palestinian audiences. I clearly remember speaking at a side event of our Jerusalem Nights festival in 1992 and telling fellow creative colleagues that we should be ready to have our own radio and TV stations because one day we would be able to get a permit, only to discover that we have the license for a Palestinian national media outlet, but no trained personnel with the requisite skills to staff it.

This idea was turned into a workshop a year later in June 1993 when Sari Nusseibeh asked Nabhan Khreisheh and me to head a media committee as part of the Palestinian technical committees. We were allowed some limited resources, thanks to a grant from Sweden, and we decided to stage a mock Palestinian TV evening news.

For two weeks, we trained journalists on TV broadcasting skills, and on the last day at exactly 6 p.m., we presented at the Hakawati National Theatre the Palestinian nightly news with jingles, news, reports, live studio interviews, and even sports and weather. The program was called Experimental Television News. At the time when interviewed about it by *The New York Times*, I said, "We're sick and tired of being the object of the news. We want to design our own narrative, our own news in our own words."

Palestine TV and the Voice of Palestine radio were born as part of the Oslo Accords. The justification at the time was that Palestinians could not hold elections for their legislative council without having a radio and TV station.

Interview with Yitzhak Rabin

During this period, I was given the opportunity to carry out an exclusive interview with Israel's Prime Minister Yitzhak Rabin. The interview with Rabin, the first an Israeli leader gave to a Palestinian newspaper, took place at the Jerusalem prime ministry on 9 June 1993 and appeared on an entire page of the leading Palestinian daily *Al Quds* on 10 June. Many international media outlets published its contents and interviewed me about the experience.

The interview was very surreal. I arrived with the photographer Mohammad Abu Khader at the prime minister's office and when we sat down there was no small talk. Rabin, a well-known army man who had called for the breaking of Palestinian bones, seemed to have felt that he had to do the interview. Realizing that he was all business, I asked if we should start and he said yes. The interview went on for an entire hour. But for me, the most memorable part of the interview was midway through when I asked the Israeli leader why Israel doesn't just talk to the PLO instead of talking to people appointed by the PLO and who you know report back to the Palestinian organization. At that time, the PLO was still considered an illegal terrorist organization and therefore sympathy or affiliation with the PLO was an imprisonment crime for at least six months. I had no idea at the time that the Israelis were conducting serious behind-the-scenes negotiations with the PLO and it seemed that Rabin was in a bind of sorts. He looked at one of his aides and said in English: "How can I answer this question in a nice way?" The aide realized that his boss needed time so he handed Rabin a cigarette, lit it, and allowed the Israeli prime minister a few puffs before answering something like "it is not the right time to do so." We went on from there to another question that I have always wanted to ask all Israelis. "What is your vision of the status of the West Bank and Gaza in 15 years?" I asked. Rabin, whose Labor party had always talked about the Jordan Option, answered without hesitation: "Some type of entity in close coordination with Jordan."

Oslo Accords initiated, opposed, and foiled

Six years of civil disobedience and protest brought about the Oslo Accords and the signing of the Declaration of Principles between Israel and the PLO on 13 September 1993. On the eve of that important agreement, the PLO recognized Israel and Israel recognized the PLO as the representative of the Palestinian people. Unfortunately, that important event, sealed with a White House handshake between PLO Chairman Arafat and Israeli Prime Minister Rabin, was upended when a radical Israeli settler named Yigal Amir assassinated Rabin in 1995 as he was departing from a peace rally in Tel Aviv.

The courageous Rabin was succeeded by Benjamin Netanyahu in his first term as Israeli prime minister. Then, as now, Netanyahu multiplied illegal settlements in the occupied Palestinian territories. Since Oslo, the number of Israeli settlers has quadrupled in the West Bank, the very territory that was supposed to be an independent Palestinian state alongside Israel.

Following the signing of the Oslo Accords, I was quickly involved in two major media projects. Ilan Ziv and I again co-produced a new documentary working with some of the same filmmakers. The new film included the wedding of our star Palestinian filmmaker Suhair Ismail and another interesting moment during the *tulbeh*, the visit by dignitaries and family leaders of the man to the family of the bride in a public asking for her hand in marriage from her family's elder men. However, there were no men from Suhair's close family setting after the death of her father who joined the PLO in Lebanon and her brother who was killed by Israelis during the intifada. Their absence didn't go unnoticed as one of the elders of the groom, unaware of these details, appeared on camera asking, "Where are the men of the family of the bride?"

Personal stories aside, the documentary, which we later titled *On the Edge of Peace*, included settler interviews as well as a number of Hamas-initiated suicide bombings that occurred as the talks for the implementation of the Oslo Accords were ongoing. It was clear from the documentary that both Jewish settlers and Hamas were totally opposed to the Oslo peace process and were set to do anything they can to derail it.

Sesame Street

My interview with Rabin and the success we had made at the Jerusalem Film Institute brought with it a new wave of interest from international organizations. One was from the Children's Television Workshop, the NGO behind Sesame Street, the famous American children's educational television series. One day late in 1994 after the Oslo Accords were signed, I received a call from an American producer named Lewis Bernstein, who said he was hopeful about the peace process and wanted to produce an Israeli-Palestinian version of Sesame Street. I was not interested initially, but later agreed based on the desire of our staff to be part of a world class production. I insisted on shifting the budget for more training and that we have a separate Palestinian show. The Sesame Street people agreed to shift $300,000 for training.

Below is how *The New York Times* in 2009 talked about the start of what would be a major media project and, like the peace process, ended up being destroyed by politics:

IN 1994, PRODUCTION EXECUTIVES at Sesame Workshop first approached Kuttab about creating a Palestinian version of the show. Kuttab was a founder of the Jerusalem Film Institute, which trained Palestinians in television journalism. Kuttab was unenthusiastic.

"We are looking for a divorce from the Israelis, not a marriage," he recalls telling the Sesame Workshop executives who first approached him. Palestinians had strong taboos against what they called "normalization" — working with or even openly acknowledging Israel before a peace settlement was reached. But the opportunity to build up Palestinian television capability and benefit from American and Israeli expertise and money proved irresistible to Kuttab.

Although most people I talked to who worked on the joint production, which was broadcast in 1998, spoke fondly of it, they said the process of reaching consensus on even small details was arduous. The Palestinians didn't want to show Israel's flag or state colors or kids wearing yarmulkes. The Israelis didn't want to see the Palestinian flag or Muppets wearing keffiyehs. Khalil Abu Arafeh, the head writer for the Palestinian show at the time, gravely recalled that "the issue of hummus and falafel was very heated." (Both sides considered the dishes to be "their" food.) The most contentious segments were the ones in which the Israeli and Palestinian Muppets interacted. Each set of Muppets lived on their own set — so where would they meet? An American adviser from Sesame Workshop proposed the Muppets meet at a neutral third location on the border of their sets, perhaps a park, but the Palestinians weren't comfortable with that idea — they wanted to know who *owned* the park. Dolly Wolbrum, the show's producer at IETV, told me she thought that wasn't a question that 3-to-6-year-olds would wonder about, but Kuttab said he felt Palestinian children would assume it was an Israeli park. He proposed dividing the park by a low wall, an idea Wolbrum said was a deal breaker. They finally agreed that the Muppets would visit one another's streets rather than meet in a park. But again, controversy arose: the Israelis were in favor of spontaneous Muppet drop-bys, but the Palestinians insisted the visits had to be by invitation only. "The only Israelis who come to Palestinian neighborhoods uninvited are settlers," Kuttab explained to me.

For Kuttab, the Israeli idea that Palestinian and Israelis on the show would be best buddies who casually drop in on each other was absurd. In real life, the Israeli production staff refused to travel to Ramallah even for informal visits — they feared for their safety — and many of the Palestinian crew didn't have permits to enter Jerusalem. "There was no wall yet," Kuttab told me, referring to the concrete boundary that the Israeli government began constructing in 2002 to separate Israel and some settlements from the Palestinian territories, "but there was an invisible wall between us, and we didn't want to give kids a false impression that everything was happy."

Kuttab told me he felt that trying to recreate the let's-get-along diversity of the American show was the wrong approach for the Middle East. The idyllic images of racial harmony on "Sesame Street" may have helped African-American children feel more a part of American culture, he said, but that tactic wasn't useful in the context of a two-state solution. "Israel wants to be a Jewish state, and Palestinians want to have an Arab state," Kuttab explained.

After my book was released, National Public Radio did the following report in June 2018. Below are some excerpts:

> About 20 years ago, the Muppets inserted themselves in the Mideast conflict. A "Sesame Street" program was adapted for Israeli and Palestinian children to help foster peace. One of the creators of the show has written a book about it with some important takeaways. Though the production itself did not survive much longer than so many peace plans, its legacy carries on, as NPR's Deborah Amos reports.
>
> DEBORAH AMOS: The surprise offer came from "Sesame Street" New York in the early 1990s - produce a program for children that brings Israelis and

Palestinian kids together. In his new book "Sesame Street, Palestine," journalist Daoud Kuttab, the head of a television production company, writes that at first he said, no thanks. It was too politically risky. Then his Palestinian staff said, are you crazy?

DAOUD KUTTAB: Yes. My colleagues, they said, this is a chance in a lifetime to work with "Sesame Street." And as a result, we came up with the idea of creating a separate Palestinian kind of "Sesame Street." This way, we took advantage of the fact that money was available to do this big program.

AMOS: At the time, reality was already changing because of real-world events. The Oslo peace accords had been signed a year earlier. For Kuttab, maybe there was an opportunity for a groundbreaking program.

KUTTAB: I was aware that we were starting or working on unchartered territory. I knew that Sesame had not done that kind of a search for solving conflict.

AMOS: You might call it the two-street solution - separate versions, one in Hebrew, one in Arabic. And there would also be crossover segments, explains Kuttab.

KUTTAB: Israeli Muppets meet Palestinian Muppets, and they kind of find some kind of a common ground between them.

AMOS: The program first aired on April 1, 1997, with original Muppets created for Palestinian children - Haneen, a young, energetic orange monster, and Kareem, a green rooster. He would teach children the importance of showing up on time, as Kuttab wrote in his book.

KUTTAB: I wanted kind of a character to be extremely crazy about being on time. Everything had to be on time. We wanted to be funny, but also, we wanted to deal with some of our own kind of weaknesses.

AMOS: And studies proved the show had impact, he says.

KUTTAB: I think what we can take credit for is that we tried to teach children respecting the other. I think that to me is the most important goal that we accomplished.

AMOS: A hopeful political landscape helped usher in the program. Eventually politics ended its production, says Kuttab. The Oslo peace accords fell apart. A spiral of violence further divided Israelis and Palestinians. In 2012, the U.S. Congress cut off funding for the Palestinian production.

KUTTAB: They shut us down, and they ended the USAID grant. Basically, it ended there.

The disappointment in the United States for pulling out funding to a peaceful children's program was the reason that I used the subtitle to my book: "The ups and downs of producing a children's program."

The downs were not limited to the lack of producing the children's program. Much more troubling was in shutting down the talks and the efforts for dealing with the permanent status issues that were supposed to have been resolved within the five-year transitional period, including addressing the Palestinian refugee rights, which could have been resolved had there been a courageous Israeli leader admitting Israel's moral and historic responsibility for causing the Palestinian refugee ordeal. Instead, Israel has doubled down and has done everything it can to deny Palestinians even the idea of having this right, as we have seen in the unprecedented attack against UNRWA that has been mandated to provide services and work for Palestinian refugees until their rights are addressed. In late October 2024, Israel passed two laws banning UNRWA, confiscating the property where its headquarters are based in Jerusalem, and announcing plans to build a large Jewish settlement on the premises of its headquarters in East Jerusalem.

Chapter Five

Addressing the rights of Palestinian refugees

The Palestinian refugee issue is very personal for me and our family. My father, his mom, and brother are refugees of the 1948 Nakba even though they never lived in tents in the many Palestinian refugee camps that dot the West Bank, Gaza, Jordan, Syria, and Lebanon. I grew up hearing stories from my dad about what happened in the years before they became refugees. There is no doubt in my mind that the pre-state armed Zionist groups were fully responsible for the creation of the Palestinian refugee problem. There are many formulas for addressing this highly challenging issue, but I believe all fail if they do not include something that is quite simple and has been demanded by Palestinians in negotiation talks: That Israel accepts its historic and moral responsibility for causing the Palestinian refugee problem.

My father George Kuttab and his mother, our Tata Nazira Fatalleh, fled their neighborhood of Musrara in what is now west Jerusalem after their sister Hoda's husband, Elias, was killed by Zionist snipers in front of her and her children. They went to the Jordanian city of Zarqa and were later followed by my paternal uncle Qustandi. Ammo Qustandi's famous family words, which were repeated in our homes for years when he arrived in Zarqa, continue to resonate and bring smiles to our faces. "Waving the metal key he said: 'I have locked the house with two clicks assuring his mom and my dad that their Jerusalem home is safe.'" It was not.

We grew up hearing stories about the exquisitely carved closet that my late grandfather, a skilled carpenter, had affixed in their small house to use all available space. Decades later after the 1967 war, we paid a visit to their old house only to see that the carved closet was taken apart and lying in the house yard. We never entered nor made our presence or our story known to the Yemeni and other Mizrahi (Oriental) Jews who were housed in the neighborhood, possibly because it was so close to the borders with the Jordanian army at the time and the fact that they were already given low priority to house the Israeli Ashkenazi (European) Jews.

Furthermore, since its establishment, the state of Israel has totally refused to implement successive UN resolutions demanding that it gives permission to refugees to return. Our family friend Ibrahim Matar, who worked with the Mennonite Central Committee after the 1967 war and was famous for his tours of Jerusalem, has published a photo book detailing the many homes of Palestinians in what is known as West Jerusalem. My dad's humble home in Musrara naturally did not make the cut. My dad worked in the city of Zarqa as a teacher and principal of a church school, and as far as I know, if he had an UNRWA card that allowed its holders to get food rations, he never used it. But my uncle did.

Despite my personal knowledge about the Palestinian refugee issue and my interactions in years as a journalist both in the West Bank and Gaza as well as later in life in Jordan, I know that the Palestinian refugee issue is not a deal breaker if Israel really wants peace. The right of return was not the deal breaker in various Palestinian-Israeli talks, whether in Oslo, Camp David, or Taba. I know from personal interactions that if allowed to choose, the overwhelming majority of Palestinian refugees – while preferring to stay where they are or choosing a third country or returning to the Palestinian state – do not insist on return to what is now Israel.

However, after decades of exile, the diaspora will not be erased so easily and the main source of frustration for a people that today numbers more than 12 million will persist in the absence of a resolution to the larger Palestinian conflict over land. And all insist on the right of return and would like to see Israel admit its historic and moral responsibility for having caused the misery that they, their parents, and their grandparents have suffered.

So, let's walk through the historic evolution of the issue of Palestinian refugees, their internationally recognized rights, the difference between 1948 refugees and the 1967 displaced Palestinians, and their general attitudes. Let's also reflect on some of the practical solutions that exist to deal with the Palestinian refugee issue within the idea of a permanent peace based on the creation of an independent Palestinian state.

From Return to Resettlement

When the state of Israel was born, Israeli militias and armed groups ethnically cleansed Palestinians from hundreds of villages and towns, which prominent Israeli historian Ilan Pappe details so thoroughly in his book *The Ethnic Cleansing of Palestine*. More than 750,000 Palestinians, who were living in what Israel declared to be its state on 15 May 1948, became refugees overnight.

These sudden refugees, forcibly displaced as they fled the brutality of Zionist armed attacks and massacres, flooded the nearby areas of the West Bank (which would later be annexed to Jordan) and the Gaza Strip (which was administered by Egypt). They also managed to find refuge in Lebanon, Syria, Egypt, and areas in the east bank of the Jordan River. Palestinians living in the center and southern areas of historic Palestine crowded into the seaside strip of Gaza. In time, those refugees would make up the large majority of its population and are yet again forced out of their homes today.

Unused land plots were given to the temporary refugees, unknown to them or local governments that this was no temporary status that would become a decades-long housing problem. Unable to return after the war because of the new state of Israel's refusal to allow them back home, the refugees lived in tents and later corrugated iron-roofed shanty homes in an exceedingly small geographic area.

Images of Palestinian refugees in the first winter of 1948 and subsequent years would be shown around the world, prompting the United Nations to move quickly to address this humanitarian crisis. The UN, which replaced the League of Nations, was intent on a new post-World War II order in which the emerging powers, led by the United States, would not tolerate such mass deportation of a civilian population reminiscent of European ethnic cleansing. The United States, the first country to recognize Israel, was caught in a bind.

As the chair of the UN Conciliation Commission for Palestine, the United States realized that Israel would never allow the refugees back to their homes. It looked for an alternative to the right of return in the form of local integration in host countries where the Palestinians had become refugees. The scheme for this, modeled on the Tennessee Valley Authority, became UNRWA.

The "Works" in UNRWA's name refers to large-scale and labor-intensive public work schemes envisaged to economically integrate the refugees in the host countries. In this sense, UNRWA was born with 'original sin' because it changed the direction of the pursuit of a solution to the refugee question from return, as per United Nations General Assembly (UNGA) Resolution 194, to *tawteen* (resettlement) just 12 months later.

Created by the UNGA resolution as a temporary agency, UNRWA had no set budget from the United Nations, and its mandate, renewed regularly, set the parameters for its operations.

The Americans and their Western allies decided to fund this new agency while hoping that its mandate would be short-lived. Payment for UNRWA's commissioner and senior managers came from the UN itself, but all other staff were paid mostly from donor funding, making fundraising the priority for the agency's top brass. As it was expected to be a temporary organization until Israel agreed to the return of the refugees under UN Resolution 194, the agency was unable to work on a regular budget to be set beforehand.

UNRWA, which has had international (largely Western) directors-general ever since it launched operations in 1950, began the effort of organizing housing, medical support, elementary education, and vocational training for the refugees. The new agency made agreements with local authorities in Jordan, Egypt, Syria, and Lebanon to fulfill its mission.

As a relief and works agency, it gave priority to Palestinian refugees themselves to work in its clinics, schools, and vocational training centers. Registered Palestinian refugees used their UNRWA registration cards at food centers, medical clinics, and local UNRWA schools.

The Nakba and Right of Return

The 1967 War represented another chapter in the continuing misery of Palestinian refugees and UNRWA's evolution in hopes of alleviating their plight.

While most of the Palestinian refugees had lost their homes and land in the 1948 Nakba, called *laji'in* (refugees), a new batch of refugees, known as *nazihin* (displaced), was created as the Israeli military rolled into Gaza and the West Bank in the June 1967 War in the *Naksa* (setback).

Many families – especially in the Jordan Valley area camps – were already refugees who had been pushed out during the 1948 War to the safer east bank of the Jordan River, now the Hashemite Kingdom of Jordan, but the dramatic defeat of Arab armies ceding land to Israel created a new wave of first-time refugees.

Palestinians in the West Bank, whether refugees or not, as well as in the East Bank, were all given Jordanian citizenship as part of the annexation of the former to Jordan following the Nakba.

Israel explicitly requested UNRWA to continue its operations in Gaza and the West Bank during the 1967 War and an agreement was reached in an exchange of letters in a matter of days.

While Israel as an occupying power did not have the right to ban the UN agency from working in areas under its control, the relationship was not always pleasant; for the most part, Israel tolerated its existence. In fact, in its years of direct occupation of Palestine, Israel was happy that UNRWA relieved it of the duties and costs of providing medical, educational, and other support that normally would be the responsibility of the governing occupier.

According to UN Resolution 194 – implementation of which UNRWA was supposed to facilitate – "refugees wishing to return to their homes and live at peace with their neighbors should be permitted to do so at the earliest practicable date." In addition to the right of return, it stipulates that "compensation should be paid for the property of those choosing not to return and for loss of or damage to property which, under principles of international law or equity, should be made good by the governments or authorities responsible." All countries, including Israel, accepted this resolution.

Plus, the UN adopted Resolution 273 admitting Israel as a member state in May 1949 because Israel had pledged to cooperate with the ad hoc committee entrusted with implementing Resolution 194. Instead of fulfilling that promise, Israel has left the challenging work of supporting Palestinian refugees to UNRWA for seven decades. And thanks to the US, even that lifeline is now being cut, undermining the critical work of the agency instead of supporting it.

At one time, the idea was that the Palestinian *nazihin* displaced from the West Bank in 1967 could be returned immediately without waiting for resolution for the 1948 *laji'in* refugees.

This idea was scrapped, however, after the eruption of the second intifada in 2000, and the idea prevailed for a resolution involving all registered refugees with UNRWA, which itself was also hotly debated. One suggestion put forward is to dissolve it within 10 years of any agreement.

The Israelis insist that whatever agreement is reached will be considered the end of negotiations on it, closing the entire file forever.

It is not surprising, therefore, that Israel would attempt to literally and figuratively destroy UNRWA at a time when its brutality in Gaza was coming under public scrutiny and condemnation around the world, with even erstwhile supporters demanding it agree to a ceasefire.

Israel has for years targeted UNRWA and convinced the US Trump administration to defund the agency in 2018 – halting 30 percent of UNRWA funds from the largest donor – because the central premise of the relief agency's mandate is the return of Palestinian refugees to their ancestral homeland, a nightmare scenario for hardline officials like Prime Minister Netanyahu.

Unforgotten right of return to a Palestinian state

Unlike the expectations of many Israelis that new generations of Palestinians will forget about Palestine, the right of return continues to take center stage at Nakba Day activities and throughout the year. Generation after generation retains memories of Palestine. The metal key representing the homes that Palestinians thought they were only temporarily vacating has become the symbol of Palestinian refugees and their right of return.

This passion to return might appear to be poetic and sloganeering, but it will continue to be a thorn in Israel's side as long as the larger Palestinian problem remains unresolved. It is no coincidence or surprise that refugee camps constitute the hotbed of armed resistance, where generation after generation of Palestinian refugees take up arms against the Israeli occupation. It is no wonder that Hamas, for example, was able to gain such overwhelming grassroots support in that tiny coastal strip of land mostly populated by Nakba refugee families.

The most logical way to overcome this popular and passionate issue and bring lasting peace is to work on providing a tangible resolution to the Palestinian conflict through the creation of a physical and sovereign state. Even Hamas, in its endorsement of its new charter in 2017, declared its support for an independent Palestinian state on the 1967 borders. Without ending the occupation and allowing Palestinians to exercise their internationally recognized right of self-determination on their own land, the right of return will continue to haunt Israelis and will be the main talking point for generations of Palestinian nationalists.

So, perhaps the best way to resolve the Palestinian refugee problem is to ensure the creation of a state based on the 1967 borders of Palestine. Unless and until Palestinian refugees have a sovereign state to which to return, even if the return is not to the exact piece of land and the home that they and their parents once owned, all Palestinians will keep the conflict, and especially the refugee problem, alive, be it in Palestine or in the diaspora. This is not an impossible solution, and here is why.

Most refugees will not return but want the right to return

Palestinian refugees who have been living away from their homes for over 75 years have already established themselves and have no real, moving tomorrow-type of desire to live in today's state of Israel. When asked in poll after poll if they would want to live in Tel Aviv or Herzliya next to Hebrew speaking Jews, almost all Palestinian refugees answered in the negative and showed no interest in actually returning to what has become the state of Israel. They largely accept the idea of an Israel within its pre-1967 borders, and, as Palestinian President Mahmoud Abbas put it in 2014 to a group of 300 visiting Israelis in Ramallah, the Palestinians have no desire to "flood" the country with millions of refugees. Two years earlier in 2012, Abbas himself declared on Israel TV that though he does not want to move back to his birthplace, Safad, he would like to visit, reflecting how the issue is as emotional as it is practical.

A poll commissioned by respected Palestinian pollster Khalil Shikaki in 2003 showed that less than 10 percent of Palestinian refugees actually want to return to the areas which today constitute the state of Israel.

The majority of Palestinian refugees would most likely want to be treated as citizens with equal rights in the countries they are in now, as well as have a right to go to the state of Palestine (no matter its borders) as a national right and if things turn sour where they are. The one exception to this rule would be Palestinian refugees living in Lebanon, who are treated as third-class citizens and not allowed to work in certain professions. For those, as well as for Palestinians in other countries, living in the independent state of Palestine would be satisfactory. Another possibility for some of the refugees is to be offered asylum in a third developed country, say Canada, Australia, or even the United States.

Moreover, the Arab League and the Organization of Islamic Cooperation both accepted the 2002 Saudi Arabia-sponsored

Arab Peace Initiative, which addresses the issue of refugees based on UN Resolution 194 as something that can be accomplished by consensus rather than clashes, unlike various attempts by Israel and its apologists who insist the problem is unsolvable. The Arab initiative states that "an agreed solution must be found," virtually offering Israel veto power over the implementation of Resolution 194 and any solution it does not consider acceptable.

That is why the first step toward any solution must be for Israel to accept its moral and historic responsibility for the Palestinian refugee problem and recognize Palestinian refugees' inalienable right to return. Only when Palestinians get that acknowledgement will they agree on a permanent solution to the refugee issue.

Such a solution could involve some refugees, especially those currently living in difficult conditions, moving either to a Palestinian state, to a third country, or – yes – to Israel. But it would also include mechanisms that would limit the return of Palestinian refugees to Israel.

That leaves two problems: one symbolic, one political. An admission by a courageous Israeli prime minister of the responsibility of Israel for causing the Palestinian refugee problem would neutralize many who have been holding on to the keys of their grandparents' homes and demanding the literal implementation of their right of return. Politically, neutralizing the demand of the right of return can only happen if it comes as part of a package deal that includes real Israeli withdrawal and the creation of a sovereign and independent, viable Palestinian state within the 1967 borders.

Revisiting the Ottawa Process

Perhaps the most consistent and comprehensive discussions on the Palestinian refugee issue over the years are best summarized in a Canadian effort referred to generally as the Ottawa Process, a mostly academic project led by Canadian scholars and former diplomats connected to McGill University. The project launched a website available to everyone, Palestinian Refugee ResearchNet, which collected data of all relevant documents, research, ideas, and proposals for solving the refugee conflict. It also included a political solution between the parties as well as individual solutions.

The Ottawa experts, who based their work on historical experience with cases of refugees, have documented in minute detail what such an approach – one that heeds current political realities and respects Palestinian needs and aspirations – could look like. They recommended dealing with the Palestinian refugees on the basis of a two-step approach: initially, a commitment from the refugees that they agree with the process and then, choosing one of four locations where they agree to be permanently settled.

These include staying in the country they already are in, moving to a third country, returning to live in the Palestinian state and, a smaller group, returning to live in Israel. The Ottawa group recommended cash infusion for the initial step and a comprehensive compensation based on international standards for the second.

Israel has so far refused to accept responsibility for the creation and exacerbation of the Palestinian refugee problem, but previous governments agreed to support any international fund to compensate refugees and to accept a small number of returning refugees based on humanitarian needs, possibly within a gradual process to reunite with their families who stayed in what became Israel after 1948. That was in essence the offer Palestinians made in 2000, toward the end of Israeli Prime Minister Ehud Barak's tenure. Palestinians and Israelis seemed to be inching toward an agreement to allow 100,000 Palestinians to return to Israel, which would also contribute money to resettle refugees and to an international fund that would offer some compensation for property loss.

You would think that Jews from around the world, as well as modern day Israelis, should be the first to understand the difference between the right and the yearning, on the one hand, and the implementation of the right of return, on the other. For 2,000 years Jews were constantly reminding each other of the prayer for Zion by repeating the mantra "next year in Jerusalem." No one opposed that Jewish desire and hope and no one should demand Palestinians to stop having such hope and aspiration.

Since the advent of Zionism, Jewish Zionists have repeatedly said that they wanted a state as Jewish as France is French or England is British. The idea of flooding the state of Israel with unwanted hundreds of thousands or millions of non-Jews is understood to be not practical and will not happen. Modern day politics and the interests of peoples and states do not and should not be run based on poetic wishes or on prayers and desires. Today's state requires national planning, and therefore it cannot in regular times deal with something as unpredictable as millions of people moving into their country. Sovereign states have a right to know what the demographics are.

However, negotiations are always about reciprocity. If the Israelis wish that none of the Palestinians they kicked out of their homes and lands ever come back, they need to at least recognize their own historical role in creating the refugee problem. If they do that as part of a land-for-peace package agreement, they will discover that

Palestinians will be generous in helping them with their own demographic problem.

Until the Israelis are ready to negotiate, though, defunding UNRWA to bring about its demise and adding humanitarian pressure on the Palestinian refugee population in the West Bank, Gaza, and neighboring host countries is only going to backfire and destroy all efforts that have been spent on finding any solution to an issue that is here to stay. The refugee issue is a raw problem that is very emotional to many people but if asked to choose between the prolonging of the occupation with the right of return as the only obstacle, many refugees will agree to forego the implementation of this right while insisting on the need for Israel to take moral and historic responsibility for it.

I have always thought that the two biggest issues that were holding up a deal were the right of return for refugees and the issue of Jerusalem. In this chapter I have detailed how the right of return can be addressed and in the coming chapter I will argue on ways to deal with the Jerusalem issue.

Chapter Six

Gaza, the West Bank, and the issues of Jerusalem

Much has been said and argued regarding the borders of the proposed independent Palestinian state. Most politicians talk about the two-state solution with little reference or explanation on the issues of the borders. The legal and appropriate answer is simple. Suppose we accept the post-World War II principles that it is unacceptable to take land by force. In that case, the answer to this question is simple: the Palestinian state's borders should be the 4 June 1967 of the Palestinian territories; meaning, the West Bank including East Jerusalem and Gaza.

The natural response is that in 57 years, a lot has changed and there are realities on the ground. Some Israelis were born, and some died during this period in those areas. So, a literal implementation of the 1967 borders means the need to remove people from their homes and towns (the illegal settlements according to international law) and rehouse them in areas within the internationally accepted borders of the state of Israel. This issue is not simple, as we are talking about 730,000 Israelis.

It is true that most of this Israeli population lives either in East Jerusalem or in major built-up areas across to the 1949 armistice line, better known as the Green Line. Some have suggested that if you remove East Jerusalem and the major settlements close to the old border, the numbers would be manageable. That issue was discussed in great detail during the interim period talks after signing the Declaration of Principles at the White House in 1993.

Palestinian leader Yasser Arafat at the time conceded that some land swaps could take place in order to accommodate the creation of a Palestinian state without having to rehouse huge numbers of Israelis. Palestinian leaders have since repeated that idea with two clear conditions. The land swaps must be equal in size and quality. You cannot ask Palestinians to concede strategic, highly attractive land areas in the West Bank for some territory in the desert, they argued. By the way, this is exactly what Donald Trump's "deal of the century" plan, suggested by the US president's son-in-law Jared Kushner, proposes in return for land swaps that include not only the border area housings, but also Israeli annexation of the Jordan Valley.

So, what appears to be an acceptable formula is that the borders of the Palestinian state should be the "pre-June 1967 border with agreed-upon land swaps equal in size and quality."

While the above could reduce the number of Jewish settlers that might want to be relocated, it doesn't answer a more complicated question: What if the Jewish settlers who have decided to live in Hebron, Efrat, or Shilo insist on staying where they are because they believe that "Jews have the right to live in any part of Eretz Yisrael?" The term Eretz Yisrael encompasses the river to the sea area, and in some cases, radical Jewish groups like the Herut party that has merged with the ruling Likud party consider parts of Jordan, Syria, and Egypt to be the eventual borders of Israel. The Herut party has a slogan that says, "this bank is ours and the other one too."

Several ideas have been put forward as to the possible status of the Jewish settlers if they choose to or insist on staying put in their current housing structures. The most appropriate answer to this is that there needs to be two basic issues to be resolved before they can stay put. First and foremost, the legitimacy of the land on which their homes are built has to be worked out. There are two potential scenarios depending on the legal state of the land that their homes are built on.

If their settlement and/or home that they are living on was owned by Palestinians, the legal status of their personal property needs to be resolved to the satisfaction of both sides. However, if they are living on state land that was confiscated by the occupying power, that would also have to be addressed within the official negotiations between the Palestinian and Israeli representatives.

The second issue that would have to be resolved is their citizenship. There is no problem in persons being dual citizens, which means that they will need to accept

Palestinian citizenship and abide by the requirements and responsibilities as well as benefit from the rights of citizenship like any other Palestinian citizen. This also means that they will need to pay local taxes, obtain Palestinian driver's license, and obey all laws. If they have weapons and feel that they need them for personal protection, they will need to register them. They could have the right to participate in elections if they want and can demand that they are protected from anyone opposing their presence. They would have the same rights as other Palestinians and should not gain any unique privileges that other Palestinians will not enjoy. In all aspects, they will have the same rights and responsibilities as all other Palestinians. They may request a waiver from serving in a Palestinian army (if there is one) or opt for public service instead of joining the armed forces of the state of Palestine. They should have opportunities for public jobs and run for political office if they choose. They certainly could participate in local elections in their community.

While the above might appear to be far-fetched, a look at what happened in Europe after the end of World War II can be a good example of the endless possibilities that exist if there is goodwill.

Gaza

Former US President George W. Bush and his Secretary of State Condoleezza Rice spoke favorably of a Palestinian state and they introduced the term "contiguous" when referring to an independent Palestinian state. The meaning behind the term was that the movement of people and goods should be free to the state of Palestine.

The concept of contiguity, however, runs into a physical problem when talking about the West Bank and Gaza because they are not connected except through a strip of sovereign Israeli land between them. Various ideas have been presented to overcome this problem, including a tunnel between the southern Hebron area and the northern Gaza area or a secure land corridor like the one that existed in Germany regarding the connection between West Germany and West Berlin. A train has also been suggested to connect the two Palestinian zones.

In the Declaration of Principles, or the Oslo Accords and specifically in the detailed Oslo Accords II, a safe passageway was suggested. That land connection existed for a very short period of time when Palestinians were able to drive from the West Bank to Gaza and vice versa. But that corridor was quickly shut down in September 2000 after an attack on Israelis and has never been reopened or even discussed since.

The Israelis have always insisted that they need to control the movement between the two Palestinian territories even though the Oslo Accords declared Gaza and the West Bank as a single entity. But before and after Oslo, the Israelis continue to insist on this separation, refusing to allow most Gazans to change their address to the West Bank if they needed to for work or family reasons; thus, forcing many who found themselves for the above reasons to be in the West Bank without the ability to return and rejoin their work or their family. This has been a major thorn for many couples who happen to be from different entities. A close friend of mine, Ayman Bardawil, met his wife Hania Aswad while they were students at Bir Zeit University, and they lived in Ramallah for work and family reasons. But when his father in Gaza was dying, he went to the Israeli authorities asking for permission to visit his ailing father and be able to return. The Israeli official rejected his request but said that if he passes away, he can prove that he will be able to attend the funeral. Ayman was so angry. He told me that "I wanted to see my dad when he was still alive, not after he was no longer with us." I knew that his father passed away, but I think Ayman was in Tunis at that time and was still unable to return.

Many argue that some of the most horrific actions stemming from Gaza, including the 7 October cross-border attack that caused death and hostage-taking, could have been prevented. The Hamas attack was only possible because it had strong popular support from the people of Gaza who felt that they were in a pressure cooker. The over decade-old siege on Gaza following earlier cross-border attacks and the fact that Hamas was holding the bodies of several dead Israeli soldiers killed in the May 2021 11-day Israeli offensive deep in Gaza territory meant that Gazans were unable to live their lives normally. Exiting Gaza became a nightmare because the European observers decided to leave when the situation became unbearable, thus leaving Gaza's southern borders in flux and eventually in the hands of Hamas.

The Egyptian government, which hates the Muslim Brotherhood and has had a hard time controlling militant insurgents in the Sinai, was unhappy with the situation, but it was unable to do anything except keep the border as tightly controlled as possible. This created a huge opportunity for corruption as Egyptian and Palestinian middlemen extorted thousands of dollars in bribes to allow people to leave or return. This fed even more into the unlivable situation in Gaza. The Israeli siege was so pervasive and, along with the Egyptians refusing to allow the border to be used to supply materials (largely on orders from Israel and the US), the situation in Gaza really became dire. No one was willing to make concessions for the good of the people of Gaza. Not Hamas, not Israel, and not Egypt.

The explosion on 7 October was written on the walls for anyone to see, but everyone wanted to sweep Gaza under the rug, and the only way Israel would keep Gaza quiet was to help supply the governing power, Hamas, with money. Since the banks were not allowed to operate due to international restrictions on "cooperation with terrorist organizations," the Israelis and Qataris came up with a plan. Israel's prime minister and the government would allow suitcases of cash to make it to Gaza with the promise that Hamas would distribute $100 bills to Gazan families to keep them just above water. It was approved by Netanyahu and millions entered Gaza reportedly to keep quiet. Israeli opposition and media have since used this to further blame the Israeli prime minister for allowing October 7th to take place.

Israel's former prime minister Yitzhak Rabin once blurted out the fantasy of most Israeli officials. He said that he dreams of Gaza disappearing. "I wish I could wake up one day and find that Gaza has sunk into the sea," he said in 1992 long before the 1993 Declaration of Principles, the return of Arafat to Gaza, his own death by a radical anti-peace Israeli in 1995, the Israeli withdrawal from Gaza after the dismantling of 21 illegal Jewish settlements in the occupied Gaza in 2005, the Israeli the victory of Hamas in the 2007 Palestinian elections, and then the longest siege on Gaza that began shortly after Hamas took over Gaza.

Jerusalem

While the issue of geography and connectivity will be a major challenge for the establishment of an independent Palestinian state, the more emotional issues of religion will be even tougher to tackle when it comes to the city of Jerusalem. *Al Quds* in Arabic, *Yerushalayim* in Hebrew, is the cradle of the three Abrahamic religions. Jerusalem and especially its walled old city is where Jesus walked and served, eventually being crucified, while for Muslims, a major part of the old city contains Al Haram Al Sharif/Al Aqsa Mosque, the third holiest mosque in Islam that has been the site of Muslim worship for 16 centuries. Faithful Jews also believe that the mosque is built on part of the ruins of the Jewish temple and insist that they have a religious right to it stemming from thousands of years of heritage. Since 1967, Israel has widely expanded the area outside the western wall, called Al Buraq wall by Muslims, after the overnight demolition of the Mughrabi quarter, where Muslims of Moroccan origin had lived for centuries.

All issues around Jerusalem are extremely sensitive and as a result, an accepted and adhered to protocol has existed for decades. The protocol, referred to as the status quo, was promulgated as a decree or *firman* (edict) by the Ottoman sultan in the 19th century. The status quo protocol applies to all religious locations in Jerusalem and Bethlehem detailing times of worship, who is allowed to visit when, what happens on a leap year, and so on.

After Israel occupied Jerusalem, including the old city in June 1967, an important yet often overlooked decision was made by Israel's top two rabbis. The rabbis representing the majority of Orthodox Jews from the European Ashkenazi branch and the Oriental Sephardi branch both agreed that Jews should not step foot on any location of the Muslim Mosque area, which the Jews call the Temple Mount. A huge sign was and is still erected outside the Mughrabi gate instructing Jews not to enter the area because it is holy for Jews. The Jewish rabbis argue that because the area is the remnant of the temple, setting foot on it would be contrary to religious belief. They also argue that the temple would be built when the Messiah comes and that humans have no need to do anything in this regard.

Over the years, radical Jewish rabbis have rejected this position. A tiny group known as the Temple Mount Faithful have argued that this edict is not set in stone and that they can make a visit to the area, albeit avoiding certain locations and entering the vicinity of the Muslim shrine without shoes in order to avoid any chance of the appearance of defiling it.

The Muslim community, of course, has rejected all these efforts, pointing out that they have been responsible for this Muslim site since 685 C.E., where they pray five times a day and that visitation and pilgrimage to Al

Aqsa is mandated in the Quran for all Muslim faithful. The only time in the past 1,340 years in which Muslims have been denied access to their holy site was during the 80-year reign of European crusaders who were defeated by the Muslim Kurdish leader Salaheddine al-Ayyoubi in 1187.

Yet the efforts by the leaders of the Jewish Orthodox majority were not only ignored by religious nationalist zealots in Israel, but it brought death and injury as Palestinians protested the Israeli police decision to allow religious Jews to attempt and lay claim to their holy site.

On 12 October 1990, one day after the birth of our third child Tania, Israeli soldiers shot and killed 17 Palestinians as a result of protests. I later worked with an amazing team of American investigative journalists led by Mike Wallace of "60 Minutes," in which we debunked many of Israel's claims to justify the large-scale killings under the allegation that mosque leaders were repeating calls from loudspeakers to kill the Jews. The facts were the exact opposite.

Working closely with Mike Wallace and the producers of CBS's "60 Minutes" program after I was asked to help them investigate what happened, we were able to look into the way both Israeli and pro-Israeli propagandists as well as the Western media work, often unknowingly, to promote untruths. It was also one of the few times that Israeli attempts to manipulate the media were clearly exposed.

The producers of "60 Minutes" began their investigation by looking at the news tapes covering that incident, including those of CBS News. In the news footage, viewers were told that the stones were raining down on Jewish worshippers at Judaism's holiest site that had forced the Israeli army to respond. The pictures that were shown were of stones coming down as the camera pans down the Wailing Wall. The next scene viewers see is of Jewish worshippers fleeing.

To add to these pictures, most television stations ran sound clips from a press conference with Benjamin Netanyahu, who was then a senior official in the government of Yitzhak Shamir, showing to the cameras huge rocks that he claimed were falling on the worshippers and causing scores of injuries. The rabbi of the Wailing Wall, Yehuda Getz, was quoted in news clippings as saying that he heard the speakers of Al Aqsa Mosque Islamic clerics urging Palestinian demonstrators to "idbah al-yahoud" ("kill the Jews" in Arabic). The lies of Netanyahu and other Israelis have continued unabated even though, as Bob Woodward says in his new book *WAR*, the Americans knew that 50 percent of what the Israelis claim when they say "we have the intel on this" are pure lies.

The rabbi knew this, he told Mike Wallace, because he is of Tunisian origin and thus knows Arabic. An open and shut case justifying the carnage against Palestinians!

The "60 Minutes" crew began by looking at the original tapes that they had received from Israel Television. The American producers were shocked by what they discovered. A clever and highly unethical editor had presented the viewers with a twisted version of what happened. In the original tapes, the camera pans down to a totally empty pavilion of the Wailing Wall. The editor had made the edit cut just before viewers could see the empty pavilion, and the next images were of Jews running (possibly filmed long before), thus giving the wrong image that the stones were literally falling on the worshippers.

Furthermore, the CBS investigators, using many of their Israeli staff, combed through every Israeli hospital and were unable to locate a single injured person among those who were at the wall that day.

Mike Wallace then walked with the camera to the Al Aqsa Mosque compound to see for himself the source of the stones. He interviewed a young Palestinian, Jamal Nusseibeh, who explained to him that the stones that Palestinians could physically throw over the nearly 20-meter wall could not be more than pebbles and nothing like the big rocks that Netanyahu was parading in front of the world press.

"60 Minutes" also found the statement of the rabbi that Muslim clerics were calling on the demonstrators to kill the Jews to be untrue. A tourist, who was at the Mount of Olives at the time, had captured on an amateur video the entire events that took place on that tragic day. The audio track of that tape, when translated, showed the opposite of the self-proclaimed Arabic-speaking rabbi's claims. The mosque leaders who had access to microphones in the mosque were attempting to calm down the demonstrators, asking them to stop throwing stones and pleading with them that their lives are more important than throwing stones.

Even when all the facts became clear to the "60 Minutes" team, Israeli propagandists continued to refuse to accept responsibility for the senseless killings. One of the funniest interviews in that "60 Minutes" episode was the following exchange between Mike Wallace and Rabbi Getz of the Wailing Wall.

> Wallace: What happened?
>
> Rabbi: Palestinians were throwing stones at innocent Jewish worshippers.
>
> Wallace: And how many people were in the pavilion of the Wailing Wall?

Rabbi: Thousands upon thousands of Jewish worshipers.

Wallace: And how many Jews were injured as a result of the stones falling on them?

Rabbi: None.

Wallace: How do you explain that rabbi?

Rabbi: It was a miracle.

When CBS ran the report a few months after the incident, they were bombarded with criticism, including by those who called Wallace "a self-hating Jew." One year later, the head of the American Jewish Committee apologized after an Israeli inquest proved the basic contentions of the "60 Minutes" report.

The incident in Al Aqsa reflects both the sensitivity of the location and the absence of any level headed attempts to ensure that holy places are not used for political scoring points.

Twenty-four years later, another flare-up took place at Al Aqsa, prompting US President Barack Obama's Secretary of State John Kerry to come to Amman and sponsor a meeting between Israeli Prime Minister Netanyahu and Jordan's King Abdullah II, whose monarchy's role in Jerusalem is referred to in the 1994 Jordan-Israel peace treaty. The meeting reiterated the commitment to the status quo and simplified their understanding with the statement that "Al Aqsa is for Muslims to worship and for all others to visit."

Dozens and dozens of ideas have been designed to find ways to overcome the sensitivity and tensions in Jerusalem, especially regarding the security and worship issues in the old city. Any reasonable solution needs to both satisfy the political aspirations of Israelis and Palestinians as well as the religious sensitivities of Jews, Christians, and Muslims. Both Palestinians and Israelis consider Jerusalem their capital. Both sides say they want Jerusalem to be an open city with freedom of worship accessible to all, yet if there is a serious two-state solution with two separate sovereign states, the idea of an open city that is accessible to the citizens of both Palestine and Israel will certainly be a huge nightmare to security personnel.

Palestinian and Israeli negotiators have found some common ground that they have agreed upon, which could be the basis of a practical solution to the complicated Jerusalem conundrum. In the summer of 2024 while the war in Gaza was raging for the tenth month, former Israeli Prime Minister Ehud Olmert and former Palestinian foreign minister and nephew of the late Arafat, Nasser al-Kidwa, discussed ideas on the future of Jerusalem, a topic that contributed to the collapse of the Camp David negotiations in 2000. Olmert suggested that the old city of Jerusalem be separated from the rest of the city and governed carefully with supervision from the relevant parties, possibly Jordan, Palestine, Israel, and maybe even representatives of two major powers.

In the fall of 2024, they issued a document that largely echoes the idea of separating the old city from the rest of Jerusalem while allowing Jewish neighborhoods to belong to Israel and the Palestinian neighborhoods to be part of the Palestinian state. According to the proposal, Israel would retain full control of West Jerusalem, and any Jewish neighborhoods built after 1967; these will be included in the 4.4% annexation. The document states: "All Arab neighborhoods that were not part of the Israeli municipality of Jerusalem before 1967 will be part of Palestinian Jerusalem, the capital of the State of Palestine. The Old City will be administered by a trusteeship of five countries, including Israel and Palestine." The ideas were discussed in meetings with senior western officials in the fall of 2024 and the Jerusalem part was the focus of a meeting the two had with Pope Francis in the Vatican in late October 2024.

But this idea alone will not solve all the problems because since 1967, Israel has built tens of thousands of housing units in East Jerusalem while not a single new Palestinian home has been built in predominantly Jewish West Jerusalem. With the absence of a detailed plan that both sides will apply in a disciplined way involving arrangements for resolving disputes and violations, the issue of Jerusalem could easily reignite the conflict, especially if religious nationalists on either side are unhappy with the new arrangement.

An Irish friend once told me about the experiences of his people. He said that no matter how long armies stay occupying lands, they eventually end their occupation. The bigger problem you Palestinians have, as we have had, is how to deal with civilians. Therefore, I attempt in the next chapter to address a human-created issue that has become a serious obstacle to peace: illegal Jewish settlers in the occupied territories.

Chapter Seven

Solving the Jewish settler problem

Jewish settlements in the occupied Palestinian territories are illegal. The entire world has said so. In July 2024 alone, the International Court of Justice (ICJ) and the United Nations General Assembly (UNGA) both reiterated that illegitimacy, insisting the Israeli occupation that has enabled Jewish settlements and settlers to exist must also end.

The UN's top court has said in a landmark opinion that Israel's occupation of Palestinian territories is against international law. The ICJ also said that "Israel should stop settlement activity in the occupied West Bank and East Jerusalem" and end its illegal occupation of those areas and the Gaza Strip as soon as possible.

The court's advisory opinion is not legally binding but still carries significant political weight. It marks the first time the ICJ has delivered a position on the legality of the 57-year occupation. The ICJ, based at The Hague in the Netherlands, has been examining the issue since the beginning of 2023 at the request of the UNGA. The court was specifically asked to give its view on Israel's policies and practices towards the Palestinians and on the legal status of the occupation.

The most recent decision in 2024 by the world's top court and the world's top legislative body are not new. We have known this for decades, yet there has been no stopping of the illegal transfer of Jewish citizens from Israel to the occupied territories. The Geneva Conventions consider such a transfer of population to be a war crime. The Fourth Geneva Convention, in particular, is focused on prolonged occupations and was issued following what was then considered a prolonged occupation of European countries.

When the ICJ was asked for an opinion on the Israeli wall built deep into Palestinian territory, the world court reaffirmed that occupying powers are not allowed to take property or move their people to areas under occupation. It is natural to expect that at the end of war, the occupying power returns to its home country and the illegal settlers who came with it must also do the same. This happened in Europe and it happened in Algiers.

The late Palestinian negotiator, Saeb Erekat, was, therefore, totally justified when he told The Associated Press in 2014 that no settler should remain in the state of Palestine as part of any peace deal.

Erekat was responding to a statement by Israeli Prime Minister Netanyahu, in which the latter stated that Jewish settlers currently living in the occupied territories could remain in their homes and live under Palestinian rule. The statement was later modified to make this issue a choice for Israeli settlers.

Except for Erekat, the Palestinian side was relatively silent, but Netanyahu's bombshell left many political victims in his own ruling coalition.

Israeli right-wing leaders called Netanyahu's statement reckless, while Israeli newspapers said that a trap intended for Palestinian President Mahmoud Abbas exploded in the face of Netanyahu's own government.

Regardless of Erekat's or Israelis' reactions to this trial balloon, the question about who can be allowed to live in Palestine is important and must not be swept under the rug.

The easy answer might be the same one that was given when Egypt made peace with Israel, namely that all settlers who we reliving in the Sinai would be evacuated. That decision involved a few hundred, most of them non-ideological settlers. Another evacuation of Israeli settlers took place in 2005 when Ariel Sharon was Israel's prime minister. But the number of settlers who were evacuated from Sinai in 1982 was 1,200 families from 12 settlements and from Gaza in 2004 was 300 families who were living in eight settlements.

But this cannot be an easy answer when compared to the huge settlement enterprise in the occupied West Bank. The numbers in Sinai and Gaza dwarf considerably when compared to the number of settlers and settlements in the occupied West Bank including Jerusalem.

So, if the world decides to ensure that the decision of its top court, the ICJ, and top general assembly, the UNGA, are to be carried out "as soon as possible," it is important to discuss what would happen to the large number of Israeli settlers.

The United Nations Office for the Coordination of Humanitarian Affairs, which documents Israeli human rights abuses, spelled out the size of the problem to the UN Security Council in a March 2024 regularly mandated report. It stated that there are 700,000 Israeli settlers in the West Bank, including East Jerusalem. These settlers live in 300 settlements and outposts, all illegal under international humanitarian law, as they amount to the transfer by Israel of its own civilian population into the territories it occupies. Such transfers constitute a war crime that may engage the individual criminal responsibility of those involved.

The size of existing Israeli settlements has also markedly expanded. During the reporting period, approximately 24,300 housing units within existing Israeli settlements in the West Bank in Area C were advanced or approved, the highest on record since monitoring began in 2017. This included approximately 9,670 new housing units in East Jerusalem.

To begin with several facts, other matters need to be cleared up. When trying to discuss the future of Israeli settlers in the occupied territories, it is important to differentiate the diverse types of settlers and settlements. The biggest number of settlements with the largest number of settlers lay in areas close to the 1949 armistice Green Line between Israel and the West Bank including East Jerusalem. And since the Palestinian negotiators have conceded at different stages of negotiations that a land swap is possible, this large number of settlements on the Palestinian side of the Green Line could theoretically be annexed to Israel as part of a land swap where Palestinians would gain, say, a land corridor between Gaza and the West Bank or an expansion of the areas earmarked for the state of Palestine. The Palestinian position has always been that any land swaps must be equal in size and quality. In other words, you cannot exchange rich and strategic land in the West Bank with land plots in the Negev desert.

In any case, if the land swap is agreed upon, then we can safely say that many of the settlers will be living in sovereign Israeli areas and will not need to be relocated.

There is no doubt that settlements and settlers in Jerusalem are a bit more complicated, taking into account the fact that the status of Jerusalem and settlements constitute the two biggest problems that can derail efforts to establish an independent state. The two issues are intertwined since a massive number of the settlers live in East Jerusalem, or approximately 230,000 Israelis, alongside 304,000 Palestinians, in 10 larger settlements and in a growing number of smaller settlements and houses taken over inside Palestinian neighborhoods.

Different proposals about the solution of Jerusalem suggested that it can be an open city with some type of joint governing body to keep the Jewish settlements and the Palestinian neighborhoods where they are.

Therefore, if the number of settlers and settlements that are close to the Green Line and in Jerusalem are removed from the discussion, what is left is a slightly more manageable number of settlers and settlements. However, the remaining settlers and settlements have two types of demographics. One demographic entails Israelis who bought homes in these settlements because they are cheaper or because they are close to where they work, including work in the settlements themselves. For example, the large settlement of Ariel has a university and therefore, its students and faculty live in Ariel. Even though the university is not recognized by most countries of the world, the university provides them with jobs and the Ariel settlement provides them with housing. Because Ariel is somewhat distant from the Green Line, it is unlikely to be easily incorporated into the state of Israel. Ariel also has many other problems with its Palestinian neighboring villages, making it a thorny issue for Palestinian negotiators to allow the settlement to remain in the state of Palestine, although it is not an impossibility.

While it is theoretically possible for Ariel to be part of the state of Palestine, other settlements deep in Palestinian areas have a different type of problem for Palestinians. Many of the settlers living in some of those remote settlements are radical ideologues who have decided to settle not because of cheap rental or wanting to be close to a university, but because they have a strong ideological motivation to live in what they consider as Judea and Samaria from a religious point of view.

There are two types even among the religious Jewish settlers. One is a relatively reasonable nonviolent type that is genuinely there for purely religious reasons and would be willing to live in peace with their potentially Palestinian neighbors and in a sovereign Palestinian state so long as they can exercise their right to worship in what is part of their Jewish heritage from their religious perspective.

The other type of religious settlers are the Zionist nationalist religious Jews with radical Jewish supremacy ideology. Those settlers are armed to the teeth and use their weapons as well as their comrades in the Israeli army to carry out pogroms, cut down or burn trees, steal olives and farm animals, and generally attempt to make life for Palestinian so difficult that – they hope – they would leave Palestine and allow them to exercise their nationalist religious ideology of re-creating the state of Judea, which could be separate or part of the state of Israel.

While all these groups have settled illegally in the occupied territories, they derive their presence from the government of Israel and demand protection from the Israeli army and help in expanding their presence. Once the Israeli government army decides to leave, this most radical group will probably cause the biggest headache and would most certainly need to be forcibly evacuated.

Nevertheless, the big question that needs to be asked is whether any Israeli Jew will be allowed to live in the Palestinian state. Israeli officials have been asked this question many times. While most have avoided the answer, Saeb Erekat's suggestion that all would have to leave seems impractical and could be the spoiler of any future Palestinian state. A more nuanced answer has been given, although there is a lot of mystery as to what could come out of serious negotiations. Erekat's answer that all illegal settlers must leave, however, is an easy reply to a complicated question.

When pushed in international forums, some Palestinian leaders and intellectuals have said that there is no principled reason why Jews or Israelis cannot live in an independent state if they abide by Palestinian laws.

Some have also insisted that for any current Israeli settlers to live in Palestine, the issue of land ownership of their property must be first resolved before the Palestinian government can give any legitimacy to settlers wishing to live in the state of Palestine.

While most believe that the idea of settlers remaining in Palestine is farfetched for many reasons, the idea that at some time in the future Palestinians must come to terms with this possibility is there.

Some Palestinians feel that there is a huge gap between the concept of a person of Jewish origin choosing to come and live in an independent Palestine and that of Jewish settlers who live on stolen Palestinian lands, and who for decades have been terrorizing their neighbors, are all of a sudden given legitimacy and citizenship.

If indeed an American Jew or an Israeli genuinely wants to responsibly buy property and accept the laws of the state of Palestine, would that eventuality be denied?

Historically, Palestinians have been open to the idea of a shared state in Palestine. The PLO covenant and early PLO leaders always referred to the idea of a secular democratic state where Jews can live alongside Muslims, Christians, and non-religious Palestinians. Even today, many Palestinians and their allies have been staunch supporters of the one state solution, in which all the citizens of the area between the river and the sea can remain where they are and that they could be governed in a democratically elected state that guarantees all citizens be treated equally. This sounds like a pipe dream for Israeli Zionists who have always called for a Jewish state that is as France is French and Britain is British.

It is true that Palestinian leaders in the early days of the PLO, who opposed the Zionist ideology that allowed Jews anywhere in the world to emigrate to Palestine, were vague as to which Jews would be allowed to live in this secular state. But the concept of a multi-religious state of Palestine has always been part of the historic Palestinian narrative.

My own family is divided on the issue of a two-state vs. a one-state solution. My adult children and my older brother are strong one-state supporters. In fact, my brother Jonathan, a human rights lawyer and a strong nonviolent advocate, has written a book detailing how the one state solution would handle the various issues.

For this discussion, those who support the one state or two states agree in principle that either solution can and should be open to accepting people of different religions or even people who profess no religion (although the laws in both Israel and Palestine mandate everyone to have a publicly stated religion) as full and equal citizens with rights and responsibilities.

A few problems will need to be resolved regarding those illegal settlers who might want to stay in the new Palestinian state. The biggest problem that will face those who will choose to stay in the state of Palestine will be to determine if the homes they live in are not built on private Palestinian land. A grace period might be given for the settlers wishing to stay to clear their name and the name of those who built the settlements and how they obtained the land. At the end of the day, the title of the housing units in which the settlers live in would have to be cleared or turned over to the new Palestinian state, which will have the right to determine whether to rent it to the current settlers at a reasonable market rate or make it available to any other person or entity with a clean record that might want to buy or rent it.

In addition to the settlement title issue, the settlers themselves will have to come clean on what they have done to Palestinians during the years of occupation. A South African-style truth and reconciliation commission might be needed if indeed some of the settlers who have pillaged Palestine would be permitted to continue to live in Palestine.

Finally, settlers will not be allowed to possess unlicensed weapons. If they have weapons or wish to possess firearms for personal protection, they would have to apply to the Palestinian government and obtain a license to carry. This license would only be issued if the person has a clean record, and it might be issued on a short-term basis and potentially withdrawn if the person possessing the weapons acts in violation of the licensing regulations.

Other problems that need to be dealt with include the issue of dual citizenship and movement between Palestine and Israel. No citizen of the Palestinian state, regardless of his or her religion or national background, should have any special preference and superiority over the local indigenous Arab Palestinians. Jewish Israelis would naturally have the full right of worship and visitation to some of their religious sites, such as Rachel's tomb in Bethlehem, so long as this right does not infringe on the lives of the rest of the citizens of Palestine.

If Israeli settlers agree to the above and decide to stay in Palestine, they should be treated equally and with dignity and rights. But any relationship between the citizens of Palestine and Israel should not give those individuals any extra rights or privileges. If they demand, for example, the right of citizenship of a spouse who comes from Israel, the same should be reciprocated to a Palestinian from the West Bank wishing to marry someone from Haifa or Nazareth.

The same applies to freedom of movement. Israeli-Palestinian dual citizens would only be allowed to bring in their cars from Israel if the same right is available to a Palestinian wanting to drive their Palestinian plated cars in Israel. In short, the concept of reciprocity must apply to all without distinction.

In a similar fashion, a Jew from America or Australia wanting to come and live in Palestine or obtain Palestinian citizenship through marriage or any other mechanism offered by the state of Palestine should accept the law of the land and cannot demand a right that is not available to an Arab

American wanting to come and live in Haifa or marry into a family in Nazareth.

Short of all the settlers leaving as part of a political agreement to end the occupation and the creation of a Palestinian state, there must be a nuanced, well crafted, and fair solution that can guarantee an orderly change of governments. Naturally, the settlers will be afraid of potential retaliation from Palestinians, especially from nearby neighbors who have been terrorized by those settlers for years. The idea of a truth and reconciliation-type of commission could be an important mechanism to help deal with the decades-old problems and anger caused by the prolonged Israeli occupation and the unlimited protection and support that this Israeli military occupation has given to the settlers by encouraging them to live in Palestine as part of thwarting the possibilities of a Palestinian state.

The complicated situation of Jewish settlers wanting to stay put and live in a Palestinian state would require a gradual approach. A short-term grace period can be offered, in which the former settlers would have to decide whether they want to live in the state of Palestine, obey its laws, and live in peace with fellow citizens or prefer to return to the state of Israel. They would most likely be allowed to sell the property they own so long as its title is clean. Otherwise, the Palestinian state would take it over and deal with it in any way it sees fit.

The above may sound confusing at first, in large part because this is a major humanitarian issue that affects the lives of tens or maybe hundreds of thousands of individuals and their families. While much of the blame must fall on the Israeli government that allowed the creation of this illegal colonial enterprise, the persons who accepted to live in occupied territories knew very well what they were doing and that this was not their land. As a result, both the government of Israel and the settlers that it encouraged to colonize Palestine have to bear the consequences of that decision, which may have been made by earlier governments and, in many cases, by the current occupants' parents or grandparents.

Nevertheless, there must be a mechanism to solve all outstanding issues that are fair and gracious. The hatred that was created by the settlements should not be allowed to be repeated by applying draconian laws by Palestine. The rule of law and internationally recognized rights must prevail to ensure a transition from illegal settlement to responsible citizenship. Those who agree to the process must be made welcome while the others should not be allowed to remain defiant and cause more damage than what has already been inflicted over decades.

The existence of armed settlers protected by an army that is foreign to the local population puts the issue of security as a major one that must be addressed. Although Israel has exaggerated the security issue to the highest degree, the problem needs to be unpacked and dismantled for any peaceful solution to work.

Chapter Eight

Security, borders, freedom of movement, and economic cooperation

The idea of an independent Palestinian state on the 4 June 1967 borders, possibly with some land exchange in equal size and value, may seem like a no-brainer, but there are plenty of manufactured arguments against it. Most of those arguments are built on emotional issues that are focused on the security of one side of the conflict: the Israeli side. Taken at face value by unsuspecting individuals, the arguments appear to make sense.

But a more thorough examination of these justifications for the failure to implement the two-state solution leads to the obvious conclusion that for every reason, excuse, and justification for denying Palestinians their national rights, a reasonable, verifiable solution can be found. Here, we try to deal with these issues and provide suggested solutions.

Security

The most repeated reason for denying Palestinians their inalienable right of self-determination and the ability to establish their independent state is usually tied to the security of Israel and Israelis. Sometimes the reasons are connected to the fact that Palestinians have conducted violent attacks against Israelis, which have included attacks and killings of Israeli soldiers, illegal Jewish settlers, as well as civilians. Attacks have taken place both in the occupied territories and within the internationally recognized borders of Israel. There are many arguments to be made about each of these categories. We will touch on each of them, but it is important to categorically stress that attacks against civilians, regardless of location, are unacceptable and must be denounced. No matter how many Palestinian civilians have been killed, the right of resistance that is guaranteed in international covenants and laws does not include targeting civilians directly. Armed Jewish settlers, Israeli soldiers, and intelligence officers dressed in civilian clothes are different and international law does not include immunity to members of the security forces regardless of their attire.

To be sure, no country can be 100 percent immune from security breaches. The test of whether Palestine can help contribute to the security of Israel could only be measured once there is actual peace. To base the rejection of Palestinian independence on the violence while Palestinian territories are occupied is not the way to ensure safety. I have often stood in front of Israel and Jewish and pro-Israeli groups arguing that in fact, the best way to provide safety and security for Israel could only happen if Palestinians have their independent state. I have tried to analyze what would happen and I have argued the following:

Imagine if you are the leader of the Palestinian people after decades of struggle. Imagine decades of fighting for independence and tens of thousands of lives have been sacrificed. Imagine after thousands of Palestinians have spent the best years of their lives behind bars and many others have spent lifetimes being harassed by an occupation force. And after all this suffering, an independent Palestinian state is born. Would the leader of such a state allow a rogue radical element to destroy this long-awaited dream? Will the Palestinian people, who have suffered from decades of occupation, provide an enabling environment for such elements? Will the Palestinian people encourage such acts against a hard-fought-for peace agreement? The answer is obviously no. Wars and occupations have forever taken place and enmity and hatred have existed throughout history. Why would a Palestinian-Israeli peace treaty be any different once reached? Sure, such a peace treaty will include compromises, and some people will be unhappy with the compromises. But any truly patriotic Palestinian leader, who along with others has sacrificed so much to reach a reasonable and fair agreement, can tell his people that this is the best deal that can be found.

In Palestinian political discourse, there is general agreement that any peace deal will require approval by the Palestinian National Council – the PLO's top representative body – as well as by a public referendum. Having reached such approval by both the official Palestinian bodies and the public at large, those who would oppose the peace deal will need to accept the decision of the majority and can oppose it politically and nonviolently, but if they insist on any violent acts, they will and should be stopped.

Yet in spite of all the above, any peace deal following decades of war and conflict will certainly require certain security measures to protect both parties. World countries can also be asked to sponsor or provide guarantees for the safety of both sides.

The issues of both sides are crucial for the success of the security part of the peace agreement. If Israeli security is guaranteed but its forces, armed settlers, or militias regularly infiltrate the Palestinian state, as has happened in the years after the Oslo Accords, then the security issue for Israel cannot be guaranteed by the Palestinian leadership.

One final argument must be made about security. For decades, Israel has done everything possible to have peace while also controlling Palestinian land. They have infiltrated strategic locations with Jewish settlers, have built high cement walls and electronic fences, and have used immense military power and force with the failed aim at deterrence. All these methods have failed because no matter how high the fence you build, there will always be an enemy on the other side. The way to have peace is to settle your differences with your adversary. Yes, it might be hard and compromises have to be made. The balance of force should not be the only determinant of the outcome of negotiations. In international law, practical logical solutions need to be implemented, but in the end, security is accomplished by a strong army and intelligence as well as by reaching a peaceful solution with your enemies.

Borders

The success of the two-state solution requires an agreement on borders. To begin with, the borders that existed before Israel's occupation of Palestinian territories on 5 June 1967 must be the basis of any agreement. The 4 June borders of the state of Israel continue to be the internationally recognized borders.

No country in the world has accepted Israel's unilateral annexation and attempts to erase what is often referred to as the green line separating the West Bank from Israel. While the Gaza envelope (where the 7 October cross-border attack took place) used to be part of Egyptian-controlled Gaza when the 1949 armistice treaty was signed, Israel expanded and took a chunk of the Gaza Strip when it ended its 1956 tripartite (British, French, and Israeli) war after the President of Egypt, Gamal Abdel Nasser, nationalized the Suez Canal. Nevertheless, the Gaza envelope is now largely accepted as part of the state of Israel despite it having belonged to the Arab side before 1956.

Though it should be easy to agree on the eastern borders of the West Bank, the western borders as well as the borders around Jerusalem will require much more nuanced agreements.

The Palestinian leadership, as documented in various earlier negotiations, has given the acceptance of the Palestinian side that some form of border adjustments and land exchange will be made so long as this exchange is equal in size and importance.

Such borders need to be clear and will require international recognition. The fact is that some flexibility will be needed to ensure the success of the project, especially when it concerns at least two basic locations – Jerusalem and the connection between Gaza and the West Bank.

Borders mean that a sovereign power has control over the movement of people and goods. This means that the Palestinian power must be able to exercise control over the King Hussein Bridge, previously called the Allenby Bridge, as well as crossings with Gaza and naturally Israel.

No goods or persons should be able to cross the border without the approval of the sovereign Palestinian power.

This will be a huge game changer as Israel has for over five decades managed hermetic control on the border crossings, making life extremely difficult for those wishing to travel in and out of Palestinian territories. Naturally, the same should apply to the Rafah crossing with Egypt and the Beit Hanoun crossing with Israel.

Freedom of movement

One of the most invasive parts of the Israeli occupation has been the tight restrictions on movement. Palestinians have no airport or harbor, even though it has access to the Mediterranean in Gaza, where it had an airport at one time, only to have it disabled when Israel literally bombed the runway and terminal in 2001. Palestinians in the West Bank, including East Jerusalem, are not allowed to use their cars across the King Hussein Bridge due to Israeli refusal. East Jerusalemites are not allowed to use the Sheikh Hussein Bridge that connects Israel to Jordan because of a Jordanian government decision.

In addition to the restrictions on the movement in and out of the occupied Palestinian territories, Palestinians face further internal constraints. Palestinians have to deal with multiple restrictions, including movement, from the West Bank to Gaza and back, even though the US-sponsored Declaration of Principles, or the Oslo

Accords, considered the two Palestinian territories as a single entity. A safe passage corridor was designated and actually was in operation for a brief period of time in late 1999, only to be canceled in September 2000.

Palestinians, other than East Jerusalem residents, are barred from entering East Jerusalem without an Israeli permit, and even such permits rarely allow a Palestinian to stay overnight in East Jerusalem. No Palestinians (except some doctors and important businesspersons) can travel with their cars to East Jerusalem. Even East Jerusalem residents who live beyond the Israeli-imposed cement wall have to wait long hours to drive into Jerusalem and those without cars have to walk through very restrictive checkpoints, especially those in Bethlehem and Qalandia.

Using the King Hussein Bridge is a major nightmare for Palestinian families, especially those traveling with young children during the sizzling summer months. Israel decides opening and closing times, usually cutting travel on Friday to half a day and banning travel on Saturdays. For an abbreviated period in 2022, Israel agreed to have the crossing point at King Hussein open around the clock, 24 hours a day, seven days a week, but this was short-lived as a result of a traveler from Nablus to Amman having to take three different mandatory modes of transportation. First, they need to get from Nablus to the Jericho Karameh crossing point, which is under Palestinian control. Then they take a mandatory bus to the Israeli-controlled crossing. After finishing passport control, another bus makes the short three-kilometer crossing to the Jordanian passport control area. Once a traveler completes the Jordanian passport control, he or she can take another mode of transportation (a bus, public shared taxis, private taxis, or car rental) to get to Amman.

As part of the Israel-PLO Declaration of Principles, the Palestinian police were allowed to be deployed on the Israeli-controlled crossing point and travelers were allowed to go home directly without having to stop in Jericho. But after the eruption of the September 2000 second intifada, Israel kicked out the Palestinian police and has not allowed them back since. The Palestinian police are no longer present at the Israeli-controlled bridge terminal, although Israel charges a high exit fee that is supposed to be shared with the Palestinian government to cover the cost of their police that have not been seen at the crossing point since 2000.

The wait across the bridge on both sides can take hours in each direction as the Israelis conduct overzealous body and baggage security checks. Forcing three million Palestinians to use a single crossing point that is controlled by the Israeli army causes major bottlenecks, especially during the summer months when many Palestinians working or studying abroad come home to spend their vacation with their families. Ensuring travel by car as well as public transportation that crosses the Jordan River sounds so normal and mundane, but for 57 years, Palestinians have been unable to use their cars or even a single public transportation means to travel from Palestine to Jordan and vice versa. An independent state in which Palestinians control their own borders with their neighbors can accomplish what for most living Palestinians today has never happened unless you are a senior Christian clergyman, a diplomat, or President Abbas. There was a popular saying that travelers from Jerusalem would stop by Amman for breakfast and have lunch in Damascus; now it takes most hours of the day (the 24-hour travel honeymoon didn't last) to get from Jerusalem to Amman or vice versa.

While the issue of travel by car has been discussed in detail here, we have not touched on the many other modes of transportation between Palestine and the rest of the world. Imagine that in the first half of the 20th century, Palestinians had access to trains that went to Lebanon in the north and to Jordan, Saudi Arabia, and Egypt in the east and south. The Jerusalem airport located north of the city near the village of Qalandia is now abandoned. It sits next to a huge Israeli checkpoint that Palestinians spend hours each day trying to get in and out of. The only airport accessible to Palestinians today is Queen Alia International Airport on the outskirts of Amman. If your flight is early in the morning or late in the evening, you need to stay an extra day in Jordan. This might be good for the Jordanian hotel business, but it is terribly frustrating and costly for Palestinian travelers. Also, if your return is in the day and you can make it to the King Hussein Bridge before it is closed (by orders of Israel that considers the area a military zone), what happens if your bags never make it? Do you stay a few more days in Jordan or do you hope that the airlines will find a way to get it to you in Bethlehem or Nablus? Or do you need to suggest a relative in Jordan who could hold your bags until someone can bring it to you?

The issue of freedom of movement for Palestinians is not a theoretical problem; it is a problem that has been going on without a serious resolution for 57 years. And this doesn't even start dealing with the even more complicated problem of the movement of goods within Palestinian areas and to and from Palestinian areas. Imagine the problems of exporting fresh vegetables and fruits, as well as flowers, from the Gaza Strip. The delays and bureaucracy not only add to the cost making the export pricing uncompetitive, but you also have a much higher risk of your products being ruined due to prolonged delays at the Israeli-controlled crossing points.

An independent Palestinian state with normal relations with its neighbors would naturally solve this problem. Sure, there might be some hiccups here and there, but overall, having a normal border with normal relations rather than a one-sided totally security-based relationship, as is happening now with Israel dictating the terms of the movement of people and goods, such issues would be easily resolved if the relationship is between a Palestinian state and Jordan or a Palestinian state and Egypt. It would be even smoother if the relationship were between an independent Palestinian state and the state of Israel. Both sides could benefit from such a normal travel relationship just like relations with any other country.

Economic cooperation

The past century has proved that in times of conflict as in times of peace, countries of the world are not islands. Everyone needs others. Access to markets in both directions provides open markets and enhances a competitive atmosphere. If you have better products at more reasonable prices, you should be able to make them available to others and the same is true for your own buyers. If strawberries in the winter can grow in Gaza, why not export them to Europe? If quality products are available at reasonable prices from Turkey or India, why not import them?

Countries also have unique products and offerings. Not every country has gas and oil. Not any country can boast of providing tourists and pilgrims with unique holy sites that are dear to the people of faith. Palestine needs to be able to import inexpensive products, say oil products, which would be able to energize industry while it can provide attractions that no one else could offer, such as the birthplace of Jesus and the Church of the Holy Sepulcher for millions of Christian pilgrims, not to mention the third holiest mosque in all of Islam, Al Aqsa Mosque, and the burial place for the family of the prophet Abraham, the father of all three monotheistic religions, in Hebron. Palestine is also full of young high-tech people who can provide reasonably priced programming and other IT services for people around the world. Having access to the Mediterranean in Gaza means that if an independent state is born, Palestinians could more quickly and much more cheaply export to the European market. Not only can it export its own products, but it can be a perfect bridge for nearby Arab countries Jordan, Saudi Arabia, and Iraq.

A Palestinian state's economic cooperation is not necessarily restricted to countries to the east. Palestine can build on years of experience with Israeli businesspersons to import from Israel both for Palestinian and other markets in the Arab world. This also applies to European and other countries wishing to export products to the Arab region, but don't want to go through the more expensive Israeli points of entry or have to pay fees and take the longer shipping route via the Suez Canal.

Today's differences between Israel and the occupied Palestinian territories are stark, but a free and independent Palestine can start closing this economic gap. Today, the per capita rate in Israel is around $43,000; in the Palestinian areas, it is nearly $5,300. This difference is part of the driver of radicalism and violence as well as the means to a dependent labor market that provides Israel with cheap labor while doing little to improve the infrastructure of a vibrant independent Palestinian economy.

Tourism is one area where Jordan, Palestine, and Israel can cooperate. Jordan has the seventh world wonder of ancient Petra, the Baptismal Site of Jesus Christ, the oldest surviving mosaic map in Madaba, and Aqaba's Red Sea beaches. Israel has Nazareth and other Christian sites in the Galilee as well as important museums and beaches, while Palestine has holy places in Jerusalem, Bethlehem, and Hebron, in addition to virgin Mediterranean beaches in Gaza.

All three countries have access to the unique Dead Sea with its heavily saturated salt waters that tourists can float on and mineral-filled mud that visitors can use to heal their skin. A three-way tourism industry could bring millions to the local economies and provide jobs and opportunities. Imagine the huge uptick in the economies of the region if there is an independent Palestinian state on the border of June 1967.

Imagine if Al Aqsa Mosque, Islam's third holiest site, is easily accessible to the world's nearly two billion Muslims, if the Gaza beaches could compete with the French Riviera, or if Jordan's enchanting Wadi Rum could provide a unique experience to millions of tourists from around the world.

An independent Palestinian state can do wonders for the Middle East region. Removing the security equation would unleash a major improvement in basic issues, such as free movement of people and goods and thus a robust economic growth that would provide prosperity not only for Palestinians, but for all the countries in the region and their people.

The benefits are tremendous, but the bottom line is that without the end of the conflict by the world supporting Palestinian independence, none of the current security-based restrictions on movement of people and goods would ever change.

Chapter Nine

The true meaning of self determination

The failure to realize the aspiration of self-determination and an independent state led many to abandon the idea. With Jewish settlements increasing rapidly, new highways built exclusively for Israelis, and a far-right-wing shift in Israeli politics, many felt that it was useless to beat a dead horse.

While this frustration can certainly be understood based on the reality on the ground, running away from the realistic and achievable possibility does not make sense unless one is simply talking in theoretical terms.

Younger Palestinians as well as the intellectual class, mostly those living abroad, had the luxury to pontificate and consider ideas outside the box. Many of those abandoning the two-state solution were doing it out of frustration and as a tactical approach rather than as a realistic, doable strategy that could produce results.

Their idea was that the two-state solution perpetuates the false concept of a religious state – the Jewish state – and only sows the seeds of further trouble down the line. They consider the idea of two states in the tiny land of Palestine, at a time when the world was moving towards expansion and widening alliances, to be going against the arc of history. They argue that the post-colonial period doesn't support plans that include the legitimization of colonial, religious nationalist solutions and that even though Israel at present has no plans for ceding Palestinian lands for an independent state, they might be open to do that. But the result will most likely be a weak and ineffective state that doesn't have the basis for long term survival and continuity.

As the one state with equal rights idea was becoming popular in academic and youth circles, another more popular term began to be heard in public protest events. Following the calls for a free Palestine from occupation, the expression "From the River to the Sea" became a popular slogan in pro-Palestinian protests and rallies around the world.

In 2018, the expression received public attention when the pro-Israel lobby decided to punish a progressive African American professor and a CNN television contributor who used the slogan in a speech he was giving at the United Nations. Marc Lamont Hill, who was also a professor at Temple University in Philadelphia, was giving testimony at the United Nations in November 2018 when he used the phrase "from the river to the sea." Speaking on the occasion of the International Day of Solidarity with the Palestinian People, Hill suggested that it is important to seek a different approach to solving the Palestinian-Israeli conflict. "We have an opportunity to not just offer solidarity in words but to commit to political action, grassroots action, local action, and international action that will give us what justice requires, and that is a free Palestine from the river to the sea," Hill said.

His words triggered a huge backlash from the pro-Israel lobby, which succeeded in getting CNN to fire him within a couple of weeks of his speech and almost got Temple University to do the same as it came under pressure from the university's donors and board of trustees. Hill was not fired, thanks to the support of fellow academics who signed a statement expressing solidarity with their colleague and insisting on the First Amendment's freedom of expression guarantees.

"Free free Palestine from the River to the Sea" might have sounded good and made theoretical sense, but it does not answer two basic questions. If Palestine is free from the River to the Sea, what happens to Jewish Israelis? And the more important question is: in light of the military, political, and financial power of Israel and the strong backing it has from the only global superpower and other western countries, how do the advocates of the River to the Sea expect their slogans to be translated into reality?

Only one of the above questions is seen to be answered by the proponents of one state with equal rights, but the second question continues to go unanswered.

One-state supporters do not talk about a free Palestine or a free Israel, which seems to indicate that they support the concept of equal rights to all citizens regardless of whether they are Palestinian Arabs, or Israeli Jews.

Proponents of the one state, including my brother, Jonathan, who has written a book about it, insist that change only happens when you dare to think big and dream. His concept is that it is important to plant the right long-term objective if you believe that this is the best goal for your people, regardless of whether such a goal can be achieved any time soon or not.

While some of those arguments have some basic truth to them, they lack the most important ingredient, namely, the mechanism to achieve the goal of one state with equal rights. Not only was such an idea totally rejected by the vast majority of Israelis, but the international community, which has been backing the Israeli experiment, has shown little appetite for such an idea.

It is true that radicalism breeds radicalism and that Israel's continued expansionism and illegal settlement activity have forced many to take equally radical, although much saner, positions.

The reality on the ground was much more subdued as everyday Palestinians were barely able to make ends meet. Life was so unbearable that many, especially the youth, were willing to risk their lives and drown in the sea while seeking a potentially better life in Europe rather than stay stuck in the current situation.

The explosion that took place on October 7th was not born that day or even months before; it had been building up for decades with frustration and the absence of any movement. But for better or for worse, the Al-Aqsa Flood, or what I would call Al-Aqsa Tsunami, occurred precisely because of the sense of frustration and helplessness.

People and pundits were talking about a third Palestinian intifada, not realizing that the form of Palestinian opposition to the continued Israeli occupation would take the form of a huge cross-border attack that would do much to change the trajectory of the conflict.

October 7

The harsh Israeli response, to their own failures, has been excruciatingly painful leading many to say that this is the worst disaster that has befallen Palestinians since the 1948 Nakba (or catastrophe).

The death and destruction that Israel meted against Palestinians have led an important UN member state, South Africa, to complain to the world court that a genocide was taking place in Gaza.

While it is often very hard to prove the intent of a genocide, the public utterances of Israeli leaders were self-incriminating enough to show intent. Defense Minister Yoav Gallant publicly declared an inhuman siege by cutting off water, electricity, and food from the entire Palestinian population of more than two million in the Gaza Strip.

The Israeli prime minister, Netanyahu, himself referenced a biblical genocidal story comparing Palestinians to Amalek that involved the divine order to unabashedly annihilate an entire people, including their civilian population and even their flocks of livestock. Israelis said that the Hamas attack on the former Gazan lands, referred to as the Gaza envelope, represented an inhuman act and therefore Israel would treat Palestinians as inhuman.

This ruthless Israeli response produced unprecedented world support for the Palestinian cause and sharply increased the world's commitment to the two-state solution. The new wave of support for a Palestinian state resulted in a shift of many world leaders from words to actions. European countries that had been waiting for a negotiated settlement to emerge in order to recognize Palestine decided not to wait any longer nor to allow one or more pro-Israeli diehards, like Hungary's Prime Minister Viktor Orban, to scuttle the will of the vast majority of Europeans. Spain, Ireland, Malta, and Slovenia synchronized their decision to recognize Palestine, together pushing the number of countries that had recognized Palestine to 146 by June 2024, but more importantly adding their names to a few European countries that have done so.

The moderate European countries (and Australia) were seriously considering recognizing Palestine as a way of stemming what they could see as the growing right-wing religious nationalism that was sweeping the Israeli government after the elections of two well-known racist Israelis. Netanyahu recruited two far right-wing parties to join together to overcome the minimum 3.25% threshold that had been created largely to keep small parties, especially Palestinians, from reaching the Israeli legislature.

The victory in 2022 of Netanyahu and his new racist partners, both of whom are illegal settlers in the occupied West Bank, forced him to appoint one, Itamar Ben Gvir, as Minister of National Security, an expansion of the police ministry. He was given the okay to create his own special police unit, dubbed by Israeli media as Ben Gvir's militias. The second cabinet minister, Bezalel Smotrich, was given the prestigious Finance Ministry and was able to wrestle control over the Israeli army's Civil Administration that is responsible for administrative issues in the occupied territories.

The Civil Administration, which was supposed to be disbanded once the Oslo Accords took effect, was kept as a tool for Jewish settlers and settlements and has become the lead agency that has been demolishing Palestinian built-up areas in what is referred to as Area C. According to the Israeli-Palestinian Memorandum of Understanding in the first phase, Palestinians will have security and administrative control over the major cities, dubbed Area A, and administrative control only over the villages that are adjacent to the cities known as Area B. Israel, on the other hand, has security control of Area B and both security and administrative control over Area C that encompasses all Jewish settlement areas and the entire Jordan Valley. Area C constitutes 60% of the entire area of the West Bank, while both Areas B and C are managed by the Israeli Civil Administration, which also is responsible for the movement of people and goods between the West Bank and Israel.

As the Israeli army was fighting and killing Palestinians in Gaza, Ben Gvir was pushing harder to try to change the status quo of

Islam's third holiest mosque, Al-Haram al-Sharif in Jerusalem. His racist buddy Smotrich gave a speech in France in front of a lectern that showed Israel controlling not only the entire Palestinian area, but also Jordan and parts of Syria and railroaded to the Israeli government plans for huge land confiscations and large orders of building Jewish settlements in the occupied Palestinian territory.

Newton's law of action in nature and reaction was explicitly manifested in the Palestinian-Israeli conflict, based on his Third Law of Motion, which states that "Whenever one body exerts a force on a second body, the first body experiences a force that is equal in magnitude and opposite in direction to the force that it exerts."

As Israel was carrying out a genocide in Gaza and stealing more and more lands in the West Bank, the Israeli radicalism was matched by equal and opposite Palestinian radicalism.

The talk about two-state solutions started to die out. Public opinion polls showed a decline in support for the two-state solution, while the one-state solution was on the rise.

Demonstrators around the world added to their general chants of "Free free Palestine" a call for one state: "From the river to the sea, Palestine shall be free."

In my regular engagement on social media, I noticed that this one-state call was being again misrepresented as a call for the annihilation of Israel. Just like the PLO's call for a secular democratic state was spun to represent Palestinian denial of the rights of Jews in Palestine, the new call was also interpreted as an anti-Jewish and antisemitic one.

I was angry because while I support the two-state solution, I felt that Israel, which was effectively occupying all of Palestine from the river to the sea, was doing so without giving Palestinians equal rights. The subjugation by Israel of 5 million Palestinians under their occupation was ignored as pro-Israeli propagandists unjustly labelled pro-Palestinian protestors to be antisemitic.

Six weeks into the Israeli onslaught on Gaza following the 7 October Hamas raid, I decided to write a story to draw an analogy of the Palestinian-Israeli conflict. Because I knew that no major newspaper would publish this story, I posted it on my medium site:

From the River to the Sea explained

My neighbor came to me saying he had an emergency and asked for a $100 loan. I had not known this neighbor for a long time, but I felt his need, so I gave him a loan. Days, weeks, and months went by, and my neighbor was not paying back the loan, even though I asked for it on numerous occasions in a gentle way. One year later, I met a mutual friend and told him about this loan, and he promised to help. He came back with a strange answer. "I tried hard, but our mutual friend was not cooperative, but I think I can get you $30 dollars of that loan to be repaid," he said. I huffed and puffed and went home angry, but then after a while, I said to myself that $30is better than nothing. So I called our mutual friend back and said that although it was totally unfair and unjust if you get me

$30, I will call off the rest of the loan for the sake of a good neighborly relationship.

Our mutual friend disappeared, and when I saw him after a while I asked him what happened. He was embarrassed to say he could not get me back anything, not even the one-third compromise that he had made.

For some time, this went on, and one day another mutual friend called me and said he heard that there was a problem between my neighbor and me. I told him, yes; we have a problem. " I lent him money and he is refusing to pay it back."

Then came the hard question. "How much does he owe you?" I was indeed reluctantly willing to accept one-third of what I had loaned him, but he refused to pay that compromise offer. So, I answered that he owes me $100, which I had given to him based on his request for a loan due to an emergency and that is what he owes me.

This answer reflects what is happening today in the Palestinian-Israeli conflict. Israel is a colonial invader that took over the entire land of Palestine. The United Nations and countries of the world had suggested the two-state solution, where Palestinian Arabs live in an independent state on roughly 22% of historic Palestine. But even this globally accepted major compromise has yet to be enacted, and instead, it is being gradually reduced due to Israeli Jewish settlement activities in the areas earmarked for the state of Palestine.

So long as the loan is not repaid and the compromise has been rejected, of course, Palestinians will insist on their rights to the entire land of Palestine, from which 750,000 Palestinians were forcibly evicted and 400 villages were demolished. The right of return has been ignored, despite the fact that it has been enshrined in UN General Assembly

Resolution 194 that was adopted back in December 1948. It stated that "refugees wishing to return to their homes and live at peace with their neighbors should be permitted to do so at the earliest practicable date, and that compensation should be paid for the property of those choosing not to return and for loss of or property damage which, under principles of international law or equity, should be made good by the Governments or authorities responsible."

Nineteen years later in June 1967, Israel occupied the rest of historic Palestine and has refused to give that back since then. Instead, it has built hundreds of illegal Jewish settlements and violated the Fourth Geneva Convention that stipulated that an occupying power is not allowed to move its citizens to occupied areas.

Also in 1967, the United Nations Security Council adopted

Resolution 242 that emphasized in its preamble "the inadmissibility of the acquisition of territory by war and the need to work for a just and lasting peace in which every State in the area can live in security." That resolution called for the withdrawal of Israel from occupied Palestinian territories (Gaza and the West Bank including Jerusalem) and for a "just settlement of the refugee problem," in reference to Palestinian refugees.

So, Gaza, which Israel continues to occupy according to the United Nations, is largely inhabited by Palestinian refugees and their descendants from 1948. Israel has continuously rejected not only the just settlement of the refugee problem, but also the withdrawal from the occupied Palestinian territories.

Sure, the world has suggested a two-state solution. But Israel has rejected this generous global compromise. And until that unfulfilled $30 compromise is realized, just like my neighbor's $100 loan, many Palestinians will insist that Palestine should be free from the river to the sea.

While the concept and idea of a single country with equal rights is an optimum solution and a worthy cause, it is not clear whether there is a use, outside academic ideas, to aspire for a goal that is extremely hard if not impossible to achieve, at least not in the short term.

A better approach, as we have outlined in this book, is the gradual method that calls for an independent state alongside the state of Israel based on the sharing of the land concept. This does not mean that the romantic and academic idea of a single state should be totally ignored or dismissed, but rather, in my humble opinion, effort and energy should be poured into the most practical and doable idea. As an Arab proverb states: "If you want to be listened to, ask what can be accomplished."

Allowing Palestinians to express their right to self-determination in the short to medium term does not mean that one is denying the potential right of Palestinians and Israelis in the future to go for one state with equal rights for its citizens.

The idea of moving from a two-state solution to a one-state solution at a later stage, provided it is the free will of both people, does not mean that this is hypocritical and trying to obtain the goal of replacing Israel with a binational state but on a gradual basis. This is not true. It is entirely possible that the two-state solution would be permanent for many years, and it is also possible that people on both sides of the divide will *voluntarily* decide to consider the expansion to one state. At the present time and at any time in the near to medium future, it is highly unlikely that there will be any discernible change in Israel.

In earlier chapters, I have dug deeper into answering some of the repeated questions about how an independent state on part of historic Palestine and alongside the state of Israel can be sustainable, representing an example of the progressive and democratic ethos that Palestinians believe in. Naturally, there will always be naysayers and people who reflect a more radical and violent point of view. In my humble opinion, when all is said and done and if a genuine independent state is offered, they will gladly accept it and live by its rules.

Surely a peace treaty that will include an independent state will require many compromises, many of which will not please everyone, but that is the nature of peace treaties. Going for radical solutions will fail and bring about even more bloodshed as we have seen in Gaza and the West Bank since 7 October, although those sacrifices have made the possibility of a Palestinian state much more real.

Chapter Ten

Practical solutions towards the realization of a Palestinian state

Wars are waged with the goal of attaining a political resolution. Israel's wars are an exception. The war on Gaza following the 7 October cross-border attack by Hamas has focused on the near impossible idea of annihilating an idea. Palestinian resistance takes different forms and sometimes fails to apply the law of the war. But international law clearly affirms that occupiers have no right to self-defense while the occupied people have a right to resist illegal occupations, as repeatedly stated by the tireless Italian international lawyer and UN Rapporteur for Human Rights in the Occupied territories, Francesca Albanese.

Israel's war on Palestinians, which has also included the West Bank and assassinations of Palestinian leaders in Iran and Lebanon, has exposed the rejection of the leaders of the state of Israel from articulating a political solution to the Palestinian-Israeli conflict. The biggest ally and supporter of Israel, the United States, has repeatedly called for a negotiated settlement based on the two-state solution, but has not put any effort behind this goal and has put all its military and political weight behind Israel. The Israel revenge war has led several European countries (Norway, Ireland, Spain, and Slovenia) to take a concrete step in the direction of the two-state solution by recognizing the state of Palestine. The ICJ has ruled that Israel's occupation since 1967 is illegal, and called on international bodies to ensure that this unlawful occupation ends.

Stemming from the ICJ's 83-page advisory opinion of 19 July 2024, the UN General Assembly on 18 September 2024 voted overwhelmingly to adopt a resolution that demands Israel "brings to an end without delay its unlawful presence" in the Occupied Palestinian Territory.

With a recorded vote of 124 nations in favor, 14 against, and 43 abstentions, the resolution calls for Israel to comply with international law and "withdraw its military forces, immediately cease all new settlement activity, evacuate all settlers from occupied land, and dismantle parts of the separation wall it constructed inside the occupied West Bank."

The world body further demands that Israel return land and other "immovable property," as well as all assets seized since the occupation began in 1967, and all cultural property and assets taken from Palestinians and Palestinian institutions. The resolution also demands Israel allow all Palestinians displaced during the occupation to return to their place of origin and make reparation for the damage caused by its occupation.

But like so many previous resolutions, this, too, is collecting dust and has no path toward fulfillment without political will by the world's superpower, the US.

The Hague-based international court's advisory opinion, however, alluded to the post-World War II world principle included in the preamble of UN Security Council

Resolution 242, namely the "inadmissibility of the acquisition of territory by war."

The ICJ also found that the UN Security Council, General Assembly, and all states have an obligation not to recognize the occupation as legal nor "render aid or assistance" toward maintaining Israel's presence in the occupied territories.

While the ICJ decision is not binding, it adds huge pressure on countries that believe in the global rule of law and the need to respect international law. The international community has ignored the tragic results of Israel's continued illegal occupation and part of the results of this abandonment is the humanitarian tragedy that the courts in the Hague are also looking into as a possible war of genocide.

Decoupling from occupation

This decades-long occupation of Palestinian lands has made the West Bank including East Jerusalem and Gaza subservient and dependent on the Israeli occupiers. Therefore, the first order of business is to begin decoupling from the occupation to allow Palestinians to live in a truly independent and contiguous state. Consecutive US officials have supported the two-state solution but there has been no considerable effort to ensure the end of this illegal Israeli occupation.

The first order of business by the international community is to press Israel, as the ICJ has recommended, to freeze new illegal settlements that have been proven to violate international law, specifically the Fourth Geneva Convention. Continuing the war crime of illegal settlement would be an affront to global efforts for the rule of law and the respect of international humanitarian law. A look at the proliferation of the settlement dots on the map shows the West Bank looking like Swiss cheese full of holes.

Decades of Israeli occupation and the lack of a political horizon are in part what brought about the explosion of 7 October. The Israeli delegitimization of every part of Palestinian non-violent resistance, from targeting the BDS (Boycott, Divestment, and Sanctions) movement to criminalizing Palestinian civil society, also played an equal part. As

President John F. Kennedy famously said, "Those who make peaceful revolution impossible will make violent revolution inevitable." And of course, with violence, human rights abuses will be committed.

The occupied Palestinian territory must be given a real chance to begin the process of independence. Movement of people and goods within the Palestinian territories -- between the West Bank and Gaza, and within the occupied territories including East Jerusalem -- are the foundations of the effort to begin the decoupling from Israeli control.

The Israeli control over the economic activity of Palestinians is not a side product of the Israeli occupation. It is an entrenched policy that has accompanied the Israeli government from its early beginnings.

The Israeli system of control over Palestinian economic activity started right after the establishment of the state of Israel. In the West Bank and Gaza Strip, which Israel occupied in 1967, Israel imposed a military rule that has continued unabated.

The Israeli occupation stranglehold over the Palestinian economy is manifested in military orders, economic accords with the PLO, and actual practices on the ground that have resulted in a deformed Palestinian economy. In this context, the Palestinian Authority (PA) does not control most of the government revenues and Palestinians face so many barriers to their economic activity that it sometimes becomes infeasible to continue. According to a study by Palestinian economist Adel Samara, Israel used its military orders to entrench its hold on the Palestinian economy.

This control over the Palestinian economy was entrenched over the years and further maintained with the creation of the PA. The economic agreements between the PLO and the Israeli government, known as the Paris Accords, created a customs union between the PA and Israel. Although this customs union supplied the newly established PA with much-needed funds, it also formalized the Israeli government's control over an important part of the fiscal income of the Palestinian government.

Other forms of control over Palestinian economic activity continued in the forms of denying access to water and land and imposing barriers to internal and external trade. Land grab and the utilization of Palestinian resources like oil and water for the benefit of Israeli settlers are also fundamental parts of Israeli policy.

Ideas for immediate action

This control has enabled successive Israeli governments to choke the Palestinian economy at will. For example, the Palestinian economy shrunk by 35% in the first quarter of 2024. In Gaza, due to the ongoing Israeli genocidal attack, the GDP in Gaza dropped 86% in the first quarter of 2024 compared to the same quarter in 2023. In the West Bank, the GDP dropped by about 25% due to the Israeli policies of preventing permits for Palestinian workers in the Israeli economy, the increased restrictions to access Area C, including denying over 100,000 Palestinian farmers from accessing their lands, and further restrictions on imports and exports of goods. And recently, Israel decided to confiscate agricultural fertilizers from across the West Bank that will also have a negative impact on Palestinian agriculture.

Obviously, there can never be a free Palestine without a sustainable and independent Palestinian economy. This must start by enabling the Palestinian government to take control of its finances and resources. A main part of this is ending the Paris Accords and replacing the Israeli customs collections with an agreement with Jordan and Egypt to collect tariffs and customs on goods going to the West Bank and Gaza for the benefit of the Palestinian government. This would release at least 60% of the Palestinian government revenues and help stabilize the Palestinian economy.

The Palestinian government should be allowed to control and use all its basic resources on the ground of Palestine, under its ground, and in its airspace. This means that Israel's illegal control of Palestinian water sources must end, Israeli demolitions and restrictions of Palestinian growth, especially in the Jordan Valley, need to stop, and illegal Israeli cellular telecommunication companies unfairly competing with the legitimate companies in the West Bank and Gaza must be dismantled, allowing Palestinians the freedom to import and operate the latest telecommunications equipment in accordance to the regulations of the International Telecommunications Union.

Energy imports are a major source of Palestinian budgetary deficits. Estimates from the Palestinian Economic Policy Research Institute indicate that Palestinians spend 900 million dollars annually on electricity payments to the Israeli electric company. Palestinians in 2021 imported around 90% of their electricity from Israel, with limited local electricity production and limited imports of electricity from cheaper regional sources like Jordan and Egypt.

In the Occupied Palestinian Territories, the total 2021 annual import of electricity was around 6,678,171 MWh, while the total consumption of electricity stood at about 6,683,330 MWh. According to the Palestinian Energy and Natural Resources Authority (PENRA), electricity demand is expected to double by 2030. This will result in power cuts as electricity imports are not expected to increase to meet demand. Thus, it becomes important to diversify the Palestinian imports of electricity and start large-scale projects of renewable energy production to meet future energy demands.

This needs to be further enabled by allowing Palestinians access to lands in Area C. Through the building of solar power plants in different areas in the West Bank and Gaza, a considerable growth in the supply of electricity is possible, especially that the PV electricity yield for fixed-mounted modules at an optimum angle is efficient, according to PENRA.

Other energy imports like fuel from cheaper resources from Jordan and Egypt are important to lower the prices of fuel for Palestinians and enable economic development of the industrial and transport sectors. This will also increase Palestinian revenues, given that this fuel is much cheaper than the fuel imported from Israel.

Although the Paris Accords allow for Palestinians to import fuel from third states, the Israeli government has put non-tariff barriers to this import entailing lengthy approval processes and quality standards that are ambiguous and hard to ascertain. The international community can help overcome these barriers by exerting pressure on Israel and providing quality assurance testing for the quality of the imported fuel.

If Palestinians take control of their resources and barriers to internal and external trade are removed, the Palestinian economy will grow by at least 35% (excluding income from oil and gas) and government revenues would be enough to sustain the Palestinian economy without foreign aid.

Multi-national force needed to begin the process of ending occupation

At present, Israel militarily controls the occupied Palestinian territory, and this must stop. A multinational force must guard the borders of the occupied Palestinian territory. Palestinians should be able to travel to Jordan and back using their own vehicles. Imports and exports from and to Palestine must be ensured without the control of Israel, except for security checks which must be restricted only to international standards of security.

For its part, the state of Palestine must rise to the occasion provided by the important advisory ruling of the ICJ. Presidential and general elections in all the occupied territories that are supervised by neutral bodies must take place as soon as possible. Rule of law and a national Palestinian strategy must be implemented immediately. Palestinians' right to self-expression, a free press, and an independent judiciary are all needed to ensure the rule of law and proper governance.

Even before the ICJ ruling, Israel's Knesset passed a law in opposition to an independent Palestinian state after the announcement of the ruling Prime Minister Netanyahu said on X that "the Jewish people are not occupiers in their own land, including in our eternal capital Jerusalem nor Judea and Samaria (West Bank), our historical homeland." By failing to adhere to international law coupled with the powerful ICJ advisory decision, Israel will turn into a pariah state. The international community cannot continue enabling Israel to flaunt international law without consequences.

The ball is now in the international community's court. The ICJ has called on the UNGA and the UNSC to ensure Israeli compliance. Recognizing and supporting an independent state at the UNSC can go a long way in helping Palestine decouple from its occupiers and begin the process of implementing its inalienable right of self-determination, leading to an independent and democratic state alongside a safe and secure state of Israel in fulfillment of the second half of the preamble of UNSC 242 that calls for "the need to work for a just and lasting peace in the Middle East."

Over the years I have spoken on numerous occasions with the lead Palestinian envoy to the United Nations, Riyad Mansour, who helped draft Resolution 2334 that was passed in the last days of the Obama presidency in January 2017. He listed the important articles that support Palestinian rights.

"Unlike UN Security Council Resolution 242, which left the issue of Israeli withdrawals vague, UNSC 2334 is clear that Israel must withdraw from all areas occupied in June 1967," he told me.

Considering Israeli attempts to establish settlements in the East Jerusalem neighborhood of Sheikh Jarrah, the resolution specifically bars any settlement in the holy city, "In addition to stating that the Occupied Territories include all areas captured in June 1967, the resolution specifically states that East Jerusalem is one of the areas that Israel is not allowed to settle in," Mansour said.

The Palestinian representative also noted that Article 5 of the resolution calls on all UN member states "to distinguish, in their relevant dealings, between the territory of the state of Israel and the territories occupied since 1967." That means no member state should deal with any Israeli institutions operating in settlements, Mansour insisted.

Palestinians have also called on UN member states not to treat settlers living illegally in the Occupied Territories in the same way as they do Israelis living inside the Green Line. Several countries including South Africa and Denmark have amended their policies in this regard, Ambassador Mansour said to me on the record.

It is not clear whether Washington or any other permanent member of the Security Council would allow such an enforcable follow-up resolution to be adopted. But Israel's defiance in the face of the world's demand for a negotiated solution and an end to the humanitarian crisis in Gaza could make it vulnerable to such sanctions.

After 171 days of a relentless Israeli assault on Gaza, the United Nations Security Council approved a resolution calling for a cease-fire in Gaza, with the United States abstaining. It is a breakthrough that must be built upon.

Resolution 2728 on 25 March 2024 calls for an immediate cease-fire that should lead to a "lasting sustainable" cease-fire. But it weakens these adjectives by limiting the cease-fire to the remainder of the holy month of Ramadan, just two more weeks at most. Although UN officials consider their resolutions to be international law and thus binding, there is no direct means of enforcing these measures. Nonetheless, the resolution can be a key building block for serious negotiations.

Hamas, although not a state and therefore not under the power of the UN, quickly welcomed the decision. Israel, on the other hand, rejected the Security Council's decision and canceled a trip to Washington by officials to work out military plans to avoid further civilian casualties in Gaza.

Member state's role

The same cannot be said for Europe, whose geographical proximity to the Middle East leaves it vulnerable to the region's volatility. But, as important as regional efforts are, leadership from global players is essential to strengthen the Palestinians' negotiating position and push Israel toward a fair peace agreement. If France, Germany, and the European Union more broadly want to show such leadership, they should start by unequivocally recognizing the state of Palestine.

In December 2014, the European Parliament voted overwhelmingly for a resolution recognizing the state of Palestine. Individual parliaments did the same. But these resolutions were non-binding. And while some EU members are among the nearly 146 countries that recognize the Palestinian state, most – including France and Germany – have thus far refused to take that step.

If Europe genuinely wants to drive progress toward peace, it must show courage and conviction. That means recognizing the state of Palestine along pre-1967 borders, thereby helping to balance the scales in negotiations and clarifying the framework for peace. Israel will object, but, as Sweden's experience since 2014 suggests, bilateral relations will not ultimately suffer when a country dares to recognize Palestine. And even if they do, that is a poor reason to sabotage all hope for a genuine, lasting peace in Europe's immediate neighborhood.

Palestinians made the strategic mistake back in September 1993 of accepting a five-year interim plan that had no end goal and without an Israeli commitment to end illegal settlements. Now we are losing the so-called two-state solution that everyone seems to repeat like sand from our hands and illegal Israeli settlers have tripled since.

As the number of Israeli Jews populating the area between the Jordan River and the Mediterranean Sea dips below the number of Palestinian Arabs, a "one-state solution" may increasingly seem like the most realistic goal for Palestinians. Most Israelis would not support such an approach, though dismissing it outright while also rejecting the possibility of two states along pre-1967 borders is not tenable.

The need to defend the two-state solution by recognizing Palestine has never been more important. Frustrated Palestinians who see no political horizon are picking up guns and attacking Israeli soldiers and settlers who have been occupying them, harassing them, and infiltrating even their innermost sanctuaries that the Oslo Accords sought to protect for Palestinians.

The Palestinian president has been resolute and consistent in rejecting all forms of violence against Israelis, but his hands have been tied by successive hawkish right-wing

Israeli governments that have been literally stealing money collected on behalf of Palestinians because they dare to care for their prisoners and families of those who died in fighting for a free Palestine.

The Netanyahu Israeli government has even removed the façade of talks by refusing to engage with the Palestinian political leadership even politically. Arabs were slammed in September 1967 when the Arab League in Khartoum said no to talks with and no to recognition of Israel, but now Israeli leaders have been refusing to recognize Palestinian national rights and have not even held a single meeting with the Palestinian leadership in years. Netanyahu has not hidden his refusal to give Abbas and the Palestinian government any authority in Gaza and has declared plans to reoccupy the Gaza Strip.

The Palestinian leadership would like to go to the UNSC and ask for full membership of the state of Palestine. Back in 2012, the UN General Assembly had already recognized Palestine as a nonmember state and 138 member states have recognized Palestine since. Now is the time to go one step further and convince the UNSC to recognize Palestine as a state under occupation. However, in April 2024, the US vetoed and blocked a UNSC draft resolution recommending Palestine's full UN membership status. And the Biden administration has failed to fulfill its own electoral promises to reopen the US consulate in Jerusalem and the PLO mission in Washington DC.

Palestinians also have a key role

Palestinian nationalism and Palestinian resistance to the Israeli occupation will not be defeated by military might. Palestinians will not surrender or leave their land.

Once the end goal is clear for an independent Palestinian state alongside Israel, the UN has many mechanisms to help move the peace process ahead, including the defunct but never dissolved 1947 United Nations Special Commission on Palestine, UNSCOP. Palestinian civil society activists along with American Jewish strategist Jerome Segal suggested the establishment of (UNSCOP-2), which will be charged to produce within four months, "a comprehensive plan to end the Israeli-Palestinian conflict, and to report that plan back to the General Assembly."

The US can make a major contribution to peace by living up to its own words regarding the two-state solution by agreeing not to stand against the arc of history. Palestinians have a right to self-determination, and they have decided, along with the entire world, including the current government in Israel, that such a right should see fruition through two states — Palestine and Israel. The US was the first country to recognize Israel back in 1948, and it is high time for the US administration to listen to the calls of Palestinians yearning to be free and recognize the other half of the two-state solution repeated *ad nauseam* by American officials.

There is so much that needs to be done before a truly independent and democratic Palestinian state is realized. A total revamping of Palestinian political process and personnel is needed, including the absolute necessity to involve Palestinians in the diaspora and especially those

Palestinians in the Levant countries and the Arab Gulf. Such a process of true democratization that must be independent with impartial international support is needed for Palestinian unity of purpose and direction, which will also rebuff the unfair Israeli and Zionist excuse for denying Palestinians their inalienable right of self-determination and statehood. The road to statehood will require some hard decisions as listed in this book.

Decisions regarding Jerusalem, settlements, and refugees are major ones that will require trusted leaders who have the support of their people and the international community. Only through a democratic process can such a leadership be reached and empowered to make the hard decisions towards Palestinian freedom. Some of those leaders might be in Israeli jails and some might be out. No one should be excluded from this process; all have the right to win over the confidence of the Palestinian people.

The international community, however, has a huge responsibility. Ever since the Balfour Declaration in 1917, foreign powers have been involved and have taken sides, largely against the Palestinian people. International powers, especially western nations, have been complicit in the denial of Palestinian rights and in giving blind support to a country that has reneged on the will of the international community, including its own promises before being admitted as a member of the United Nations. Israel was repeatedly given a pass, often due to domestic lobbies, but also due to being fooled by the Israeli propaganda and the post holocaust narrative.

The genocidal war by Israel in revenge for the cross-border attack on 7 October has not only been extremely disproportionate but has violated all international norms. To be able to accomplish the goal of a Palestinian state, a convergence of Palestinian rethinking is needed as well as serious effort by the world community to bring this conflict to an end by means of a political solution. It will not be easy on either front, but it is a doable proposition that must involve all.

The time for a solution is now. Recognizing Palestine on the 4 June 1967 borders and allowing the genuine representatives of the state of Palestine to negotiate all outstanding issues with the Israelis' representatives is the way out of this century old war. It all starts with the clear recognition of the state of Palestine NOW.

<u>**Resources**</u>

Chapter One

Washington Post Opinion: The lesson from the Hamas attack: The U.S. should recognize a Palestinian state

https://www.washingtonpost.com/opinions/2023/10/09/gaza-war-israel-palestinians-recognition/

Kuttab brothers debate the future of Palestine on YouTube

https://www.youtube.com/watch?v=soz0lt6PDrU

Transcripts of the debate nonviolence international

https://www.nonviolenceinternational.net/kuttabbrothers

https://www.daoudkuttab.com/articles/1585/#more-1585

https://www.arabnews.com/node/2448026

https://web.archive.org/web/20110805192136/http://www.un.int/wcm/content/site/palestine/ca

che/offonce/pid/12354;jsessionid=ED2AC7E70A
82F5C7CCB42BC6357FCDEC

Chapter Two

https://www.britannica.com/biography/Hussein
-ibn-Ali

https://www.britannica.com/event/Balfour-
Declaration

https://www.britannica.com/topic/Irgun-Zv

https://www.thecairoreview.com/book-
reviews/the-hundred-years-war

https://www.palquest.org/en/biography/9837/iz
zeddin-al-qassam

https://en.wikipedia.org/wiki/Izz_ad-Din_al-
Qassam

https://en.wikipedia.org/wiki/King_David_Hotel_
bombing

https://en.wikipedia.org/wiki/Semiramis_Hotel_
bombing

Chapter Four

https://www.jordantimes.com/opinion/daoud-
kuttab/my-encounter-arafat%E2%80%99

https://www.latimes.com/opinion/story/2023-12-12/antisemitism-elise-stefanik-genocide-intifada-college-presidents

https://www.nytimes.com/2009/10/04/magazine/04sesame-t.html

https://www.npr.org/2018/06/26/623646528/the-legacy-of-an-israeli-palestinian-sesame-street

https://www.theatlantic.com/international/archive/2012/12/are-the-palestinians-ready-to-share-a-state-with-jordan/266634/

https://www.jerusalemstory.com/en/blog/perspective-israels-war-independent-palestinian-media-goes-back-decades#references-item-4

https://www.jerusalemstory.com/en/lexicon/oslo-accords

Chapter Seven

https://www.icj-cij.org/sites/default/files/case-related/186/186-20230117-REQ-01-00-EN.pdf

Chapter Ten

https://www.icj-cij.org/sites/default/files/case-related/186/186-20240719-adv-01-00-en.pdf

https://libcom.org/article/political-economy-west-bank-1967-1987-peripheralisation-development-adel-samara

http://www.pipa.ps/page.php?id=1bac35y1813557Y1bac35

https://www.timesofisrael.com/liveblog_entry/palestinian-economy-contracts-by-35-in-first-quarter-of-2024-amid-war/

https://www.pcbs.gov.ps/portals/_pcbs/PressRelease/Press_En_QNA2024Q1E.pdf

https://www.state.gov/reports/2024-investment-climate-statements/west-bank-and-gaza/

https://www.nrc.no/globalassets/pdf/reports/area-c-is-everything/area-c-is-everything-v2.pdf

https://d3o3cb4w253x5q.cloudfront.net/media/documents/Abbas_PFU_Edited_Transcript_1.pdf

In Arabic:
https://www.aljazeera.net/ebusiness/2024/7/10/%D8%A7%D9%84%D8%A7%D8%AD%D8%AA%D9%84%D8%A7%D9%84-%D8%A7%D9%84%D8%A5%D8%B3%D8%B1%D8%A7%D8%A6%D9%8A%D9%84%D9%8A-

%D9%8A%D8%B3%D8%AA%D9%88%D9%84%
D9%8A-%D8%B9%D9%84%D9%89

https://www.elibrary.imf.org/configurable/conte
nt/book$002f9781589060357$002fch04.xml?t:a
c=book%24002f9781589060357%24002fch04.x
ml

https://documents1.worldbank.org/curated/en/
993031473856114803/pdf/104263-REVISED-
title-a-little-different-WP-P150798-NOW-OUO-
9.pdf

https://www.pcbs.gov.ps/Portals/_Rainbow/Doc
uments/Energy_imports%202021_1A.htm

https://thisweekinpalestine.com/wp-
content/uploads/2021/01/002.pdf

https://documents1.worldbank.org/curated/en/
257131468140639464/pdf/Area-C-and-the-
future-of-the-Palestinian-economy.pdf

https://www.aljazeera.com/news/2024/3/25/isr
aels-war-on-gaza-list-of-key-events-day-171

https://edition.cnn.com/2024/03/26/middleeast
/israel-gaza-ceasefire-un-resolution-war-
impact-intl/index.html

https://news.un.org/en/story/2024/03/1147931

https://www.reuters.com/world/middle-east/un-security-council-demands-immediate-ceasefire-gaza-2024-03-25/

https://www.washingtonpost.com/national/2024/03/25/israel-hamas-war-latest-03-25-2024/6540c704-ea77-11ee-8f2c-380a821c02db_story.html

https://www.bbc.com/news/world-middle-east-68662118

https://www.europarl.europa.eu/news/en/press-room/20141212IPR01105/european-parliament-resolution-on-recognition-of-palestine-statehood

https://www.reuters.com/article/us-mideast-palestinians-germany-idUSKCN0J51ZJ20141121/

http://www.xinhuanet.com/english/2017-12/22/c_136846189.htm

https://pcpsr.org/en/node/819

https://www.ochaopt.org/content/west-bank-witnesses-largest-demolition-years

https://www.theguardian.com/world/2014/oct/30/sweden-officially-recognises-state-palestine

https://www.timesofisrael.com/pas-abbas-condemns-tel-aviv-terror-shooting-were-all-striving-for-stability/

https://www.i24news.tv/en/news/israel/diplomacy/1657098483-lapid-not-planning-to-meet-abbas-but-won-t-rule-it-out

https://worldpopulationreview.com/country-rankings/countries-that-recognize-palestine

https://press.un.org/en/2024/sc15670.doc.htm

ACKNOWLEDGMENTS

This book is an accumulation of my thoughts and wishes as well as those of many in Palestine and around the world as we watched in horror what was happening to our homeland.

I tried to write this book in an easy-to-read style and left footnotes and citations till the end. I have decided to take the unorthodox track of self-publishing this book because of the urgency of the situation and my belief that it is important to put out the arguments as soon as possible to cut off those who continue to deny Palestinians the basic right of self-determination and statehood.

By avoiding the publishing route, I might have saved time, but I probably sacrificed a few things in the content, direction, and overall approach. Some of my best friends who read the book have told me I have two books in one. I am sure a publisher would have made a similar comment. But I decided to go ahead and self-publish anyway, knowing that it is important for these arguments to be out in the public domain. Alexander McNabb, my dear friend in Dubai, encouraged me to self-publish and answered my concerns by saying that at any time in the future, a publisher could take the manuscript and work it through the proper routine. His encouragement has let me overcome my own apprehensions to go ahead and publish myself.

My editor Sana Abdallah was gracious and kind to help edit and proofread my manuscript in record time. Her suggestions and corrections were always to the point making my text a much better to read.

I appreciate her dedication and careful editing. I take full responsibility for the content of the book, and any mistakes or bad judgments are totally mine.

My colleague Mohammad Ersan helped me find my way through the maze of Amazon self-publishing and the talented Heba Sarhan was patient with my constant changes of ideas as she designed a beautiful front and back cover of the book in record time.

Special thanks to my dear friend in Nazareth, Botrus Mansour, who read the book after seeing his daughter receive her PhD in England. Also special thanks to my colleague in Washington, Zachary Bampton, who was one of the best interns that I worked with in Jordan now working with National Endowment for Democracy in Washington.

Both took time out of their busy schedule to read the manuscript and provide valuable suggestions.

I tried to adjust the manuscript with as many of the comments that I received from them and others.

In the end, I decided to move on with the publishing as the war on Gaza continued without any discussions of the political rights of Palestinians.

My dear wife Salam had to endure my physical presence in the same house amid my social absence as I tried to finish this book in record time. I owe her a huge debt and promise that once the book is out, I will do my best to be a more socially presence and responsive husband.

* 9 7 9 8 3 0 0 0 3 4 1 6 0 *